DATE DUE	DATE DUE	DATE DUE

ESSENTIAL GUIDE TO
GUIDE TO

APPLE
COMPUTERS
IN LIBRARIES

VOLUME 4
SOFTWARE FOR
LIBRARY APPLICATIONS

BY PATRICK R. DEWEY

MECKLER CORPORATION

Essential Guide to Apple Computers In Libraries

Volume 4
Software for
Library Applications

Essential Guide
to Apple Computers in Libraries

Series Editor: Jean Armour Polly
Series ISBN 0-88736-048-3

Volume 1: Public Technology: The Library Public Acces
Computer
ISBN 0-88736-049-1

Volume 2: Hardware: Set-up and Expansion
ISBN 0-88736-075-0

Volume 3: Communications and Networking
ISBN 0-88736-076-9

Volume 4: Software for Library Applications
ISBN 0-88736-077-7

Volume 5: The Library Macintosh
ISBN 0-88736-078-5

Essential Guide to Apple Computers In Libraries

Volume 4
Software for
Library Applications

by
Patrick R. Dewey

Meckler Corporation

Library of Congress Cataloging-in-Publication Data
(Revised for vol. 4)

Essential guide to Apple computers in libraries.

Edited by Jean Armour Polly.
Includes indexes.
Contents: 1. Public technology : the library publi
access computer / by Jean Armour Polly -- --v.
Software for library applications / by Patrick R. Dewey.
1. Libraries--Automation. 2. Microcomputers--Librar
applications. 3. Apple computer--Programming.
Library science--Data processing. I. Polly, Jean Armou
II. Dewey, Patrick R., 1949- .
Z678.9.E85 1986 025.3'028'5 86-17929
ISBN 0-88736-048-3 (set)
ISBN 0-88736-077-7 (v.4)

Meckler Corporation, 11 Ferry Lane West, Westport, C
06880
Meckler Ltd., 3 Henrietta Street, London WC2E 8LU, UK

Printed on acid-free paper and bound in the United Stat
of America

This book is for
Amoes Hunt
and
Ken Yamashita
Good friends during good times.

TABLE OF CONTENTS

PREFACE

n 1977, I began the quest for a "personal computer," not quite knowing what a computer was, let alone a "personal" one. After some months of vigorous examination and investigation of the few that were on the market at that time, I settled on one that was promised but never delivered. I finally cancelled my order. A few others, including the Sorcerer (the salesman would supposedly bring the product to your home for demo, but he never showed up), did not pan out either. I finally chose the Apple II (not a II+, but a II which I later converted to a II+ myself by purchasing chips through the mail and installing them).

I got my original Apple from a firm that sold electric organs--Apples were a sideline. It is still easy to recall the reverence with which I and everyone else held this marvel. The machine I took home had 16K memory, no disk drives, and programs were stored using a tape recorder. Since then, I have purchased a later model II+, a IIc, and an IBM compatible (a Zenith 148 with a built-in 20-megabyte hard drive).

Micros can get into the blood, but while you may not become a "hacker," (computer fanatic), you will find them great tools for automating many traditional and tedious library chores. You can spend your time doing more important things. If you write (and what librarian doesn't at least attend to countless memos, letters, reports), a word processing package may become your new best friend. Budget packages may save you time trying to decide "what if" questions about where to spend money in the coming year. Many libraries do mass mailings, so a computer is perfect for updating, and printing multiple copies of mailing lists on demand.

Even without these more powerful programs that are used by the mainstream of microcomputer users, there is a mass of library-specific software, generated for a very specialized market. These are catalog-card production,

bibliography, serial, interlibrary loan, and other types o
library chores. Even library instruction has bee
computerized.

None of this is without effort. The micro must b
maintained, the software selected, organized, and cared for
Staff may be reluctant to learn new skills (some wil
refuse). Furthermore, some people expect a micro to d
everything. Unfortunately, a micro can only do one thin
at a time, and each thing it does must be learned, planned
for, and carried out by the staff. Despite all these pitfalls
the literature is repleat with innovative and successful use
of micros in libraries.

ACKNOWLEDGEMENTS

wish to thank Kris Flanders for her help in making
xamples of many of the Print Shop and other graphics
rograms; vendors for sending catalogs and illustrations.

INTRODUCTION

This book provides three resources: citations for further research (articles and software directories), specific information and descriptions about more than one hundred software packages for use on the Apple II series of microcomputer, and some fundamental guidelines for selecting and using software. Clearly, software use and selection also requires a hands-on approach. Readers should be aware that only by actually using their computer and experimenting with software packages will they develop expertise.

Software for most library-related areas is included in this book: acquisitions and cataloging, desktop publishing, word processing, database management, as well as some programs specifically intended for use with library patrons, such as one which assists in the teaching of signing. Other programs will assist in the production of public relations materials (e.g., *The Print Shop*: flyers, posters, banners, etc.).

What is Software?

In order for anyone to select and use software properly, it is important to have at least a passing acquaintance with the microcomputer. The microcomputer (or any computer, for that matter) is made up of hardware and software. The hardware is the physical parts that one can see and touch--the keyboard, the monitor, the chips, etc. Hardware only changes when the operator or service technician pulls something out with their fingers and replaces it with something else.

Software is similar to our own minds or thoughts, at least in the sense that it is intangible. We can only see it on the computer screen or monitor, since it is the set of instructions that tell the hardware what to do. Such code is divided into programs and data. Data is similar to raw material that is waiting for processing by the program. Once data has been processed, it may be stored in disk drives (mass storage devices which will hold large amounts of data until needed) or even sent over the telephone lines with the aid of a modem (basically, a device for translating the binary code of the computer into the analog code of the telephone line and back again). Data may also be printed out on a printer, in either black and white or, if the printer has the capability, in color.

The fact that anyone can program a computer to do something unique is what makes it so wondrous. This creates a machine which changes its character or nature each time its instructions change. With the purchase of a program for making catalog cards, we have a machine which will maintain acquisitions records. If we purchase a word processor, we have a replacement for the typewriter. If a database manager is included we can make automated files.

Software Selection--A Process

What constitutes a well-rounded or proper software collection? This is a question which each individual library must answer for itself, since all libraries are different. There is no "best" catalog card program, though a library will find that one or the other package will do the job to a greater or lesser extent than another. Some libraries require more sophistication in word processing, budgeting preparation, and catalog card production, to name a few areas, while some libraries require only the barest of computer needs.

This gives us our first rule or guideline; it is necessary to match needs with a specific software package. No one should purchase a program because someone else found it terrific. The question we should ask is "Under what conditions was it terrific?" Two libraries may have totally different needs and, as a result, purchase two different programs. An obvious question is "Why not buy the most sophisticated package? What can it hurt?" A good question, but one of the central reasons that so many micros sit collecting dust, is that the owners purchased software that, while sophisticated, was too complicated to learn in a particular work environment.

There are three main steps to software selection: determining needs, finding software that attempts to satisfy those needs, and determining which of the available software does the job best. This last one is the most difficult, especially since it entails either reading reviews, or obtaining demo or review copies. This is usually difficult, not to mention time consuming. In some cases, it is good to check with colleagues, if possible, before the purchase of an expensive package. It is also important to be aware that, while we can point to a list of criteria or selection steps, it is going to be rare that each and every step can be followed. We may on occasion have to "take a chance," even if calculated.

Some simple steps:

1. Formulate needs;
2. Read reviews;
3. Search software directories;
4. Appraise usefulness of available software;
   A. Obtain demo copies whenever possible;
   B. Check with colleagues or user groups;
   C. Check for specific criteria (below).

Formulating needs can be tricky, but it begins with a simple evaluation of what the computer is intended to do. The specific needs of the library should be noted. Carefully evaluate what kind of formatting, standards, baud, or other requirements are needed. This is not to be done in a vacuum, but in consultation with the rest of the staff, especially those who will be using the computer or have responsibility for the work that is being considered for computerization.

The kinds of software discussed in this book--library specific software--will never be found in mainstream software selection tools: computer magazines and journals, software directories, etc. Specific tools do exist for the library community, and some are listed in this book. Reviews are now printed just about everywhere, though finding one about a specific piece of software can take time. Library Literature, ERIC, and other sources can provide access. A continuing source of reviews is *Small Computers In Libraries, Booklist, Library Software Review* and the Library Computing supplement in *LJ.*

The software directory is one of the best sources of information. Some provide reviews, but most merely repeat vendor information. Even so, it is still enormously valuable to have so much data gathered together in one place for quick comparison of hardware requirements, and important functions.

Demo copies, and sometimes review copies, are available from some publishers. They are sometimes free, though very often the demo copies are sold for five dollars or so. Usually such packages are merely limited in their capacity or may not contain all functions. If $25 or more is requested, it is often possible to apply this toward purchase of the full package later.

User groups are merely associations for the sharing of information, ideas, and problem solving. While a lot of these groups (sometimes called clubs) exist, many local library groups have been created to deal with library-related problems. Such a group does not exist in every locality, so another approach is to take matters into your hands if necessary by conducting a survey of what libraries in your system or state are doing.

A good example of this was the survey taken at the Suburban Library System (Illinois) (appended). Such a survey is easy to conduct, yet it provides a wealth of material for many people. It is also easy to keep updated. A paper copy is best since most people thinking of buying a micro or a software package do not have access to a micro and modem should the survey results be placed online instead of distributed.

Things to Look for in Programs--Specific Criteria

The criteria used for software selection largely depends upon the use and type of program. Many catalog card programs do nothing more than the basic function of input/output. The user inputs the book title, author, and other bibliographic facts, and a simple catalog card, based on some type of recognized standard is produced. Fields, capacity, and hard-drive compatibility are also important, if needed. Some catalog card programs will integrate with other types of programs, use MARC record format, download, etc. There will be a corresponding difference in price, too, which can range from $40 to hundreds of dollars.

There are many things to consider when selecting software. Some of the most important can be grouped under the following categories:

Capacity means that the program will accommodate enough records or text or whatever the program is working on.

Ease of use is determined by how long it takes to learn to use the program. Such learning can be facilitated with online help menus, tutorials, and good manuals--all of which must be examined, if possible.

Flexibility is the amount of customizing that can be performed. Two programs which may perform the same basic task, may still vary tremendously in how they do it. Some programs allow for the bypassing of unused fields, or permit several types of data entry or custom data forms.

Formatting options include the ability to change the page length or width, add or delete fields in a record, or to format to the screen as "What you see is what you get."

Graphics are important in programs which create flyers, make posters, etc. Clip art may often be purchased separately.

Telecommunications includes such things as the bau rate, preparing a search offline, etc.

Add-on products provide a wealth of enhancements an may make it less likely that the user will outgro the product soon.

Installation and Maintenance Considerations

Some of the questions that should be asked in order t ensure compatibility include:

1. Does it permit installation on a hard disk?
2. Does it come with or permit the creation of backup disk?
3. Will it work with the hardware (color printe monitor, etc.) that the library owns?
4. Is it compatible with the available DOS?
5. Does it support the necessary baud?
6. Does the computer have enough RAM to accom modate the program?
7. Does the local vendor provide any type of assis tance?
8. Does the manufacturer provide any type of tele phone assistance?

A Little Apple History

Apple Computer has a history just as rich and varied a IBM or any computer. It certainly is a phenomonon, havin sprouted, literally, from a garage to a billion dolla corporation. The original Apple, brought out in 1976, had wooden case. The second version, the Apple II, cam housed in a sleek, futuristic metal and plastic frame. Th first systems were expensive (at least by today' standards), about one thousand dollars for just 16K. To ad an additional 16 "K," if purchased from Apple, it wa approximately $200 extra. The systems did not even com with lowercase (it cost $45, and had to be purchased fron a separate company). Disk drives were over $600. Softwar was scarce. The new updated IIe model finally arrived and it had almost everything: upper/lowercase, 128K, better keyboard, etc. One thing that it did not come with was a large memory, but the memory cards already mentioned finally broke that barrier, too. The new IIgs (Granny Smith) comes with 256K, expandable to 512K.

The best Apple history book is by Michael Moritz: *The Little Kingdom* (Morrow, 1984).

About Prices and Places

Most software must be be purchased through the mail, since computer stores will carry only a few of the more than 100,000 programs available to microcomputer owners. The same goes for nearly all library-specific software.

The Apple Environment

Apple computer has a vast following, and if you are using or intend to use an Apple for library work, you are also in good company, since according to which surveys you read, anywhere from 58.8%[1] to 73.6%[2] of libraries now own at least one Apple, compared with 12.2% and 45.5%, respectively, for the IBM. The large numbers of devoted followers generate a market that has attracted many secondary manufacturers to create an endless number of peripheral items (add-ons), user groups, and enough books and magazines about Apples to fill a small library. While there are now large followings for the IBM, it is more recent, not stretching over nearly a full decade as with the Apple.

Apple, more than any other computer, is expandable. With its many slots for peripherals, it can be modified almost infinitely. In addition, there is a galaxy of printers, modems, and other devices that already exist for the Apple. If you can think of it, chances are that someone else has already thought of it and then developed it.

It is often said (though usually by IBM owners) that

the Apple is inferior because it lacks sufficient RA
(Random-Access Memory), has a "toy" keyboard, and wi
not run many of the superior applications programs. Wha
do Apple owners say in return? "Times have changed!" Th
RAM "barrier" has been broken (it is now possible t
upgrade an Apple II to seven megabytes of internal RA
storage), the keyboard on the IIe has been improved (it
even possible to purchase a large IBM-like keyboard f
the Apple), and Apple has many software packages that a
excellent and only available for the Apple. It is true th
there are a few advanced applications that are on
available on the IBM, but fewer and fewer. If more powe
is needed, the new Apple IIgs, or the Macintosh are al
available. There is no need for the devoted and faithf
Apple user to go outside the Apple family of computers.

RAM Cards

The Apple no longer lags behind with RAM, either. A
important breakthrough is the recently introduced RAMcar
capable of up to eight megabytes of storage space. Th
typical IBM PC can be stuffed with 640K or more of dis
space (748K in the case of the Zenith). These cards a
important for any application that will be handling larg
amounts of data. In the old days (pre-RAM cards), th
largest amount of RAM storage space was 64K.

One RAMcard, and perhaps the most popular
RAMworks, which currently costs around $369 for on
megabyte.

Clock cards are also important, especially if you wan
ProDOS and certain peripherals to automatically date an
time stamp files (a handy and convenient way to check ou
the last time you worked on a file or the last revision).
clock that is compatible with IIe and II+, and which
ready to go (in most cases) after being inserted into th
Apple is Timemaster H.O. (Applied Engineering), and come
with a full range of utility programs. This clock is als
equipped to work with both ProDOS and DOS 3.3 versior
of *AppleWriter* IIe. It also comes with its own powe
supply (nickel-cadmium battery) in case of power outag

ther clocks, notably the CCS clock, requires the user to urchase and maintain their own battery, and that rograms listed in the documentation be manually keyed in order to set the time--not very convenient. Other opular clocks are the Thunderclock and the ProClock.

Reinkers

ne of the tradeoffs of reinking ribbons is spots and ains; periodically, someone must don an apron, remove ic ribbon, affix it to the reinker, and replace it once inked. This only applies to cloth ribbons, of course, since arbon-backed ribbons cannot be reinked. A single ribbon ay last for years under moderate use, and under heavy se a savings of hundreds of dollars might be realized in a ear.

Ink may be purchased in several ways, including two nd a half ounce pints. The ink is poured into a small eservoir and soaked up by a felt cup. The ribbon cartridge attached to a motorized spindle which pulls the ribbon round the felt cup. Reinking usually takes about fifteen inutes, and the ribbon should be allowed to stand vernight, longer if possible. If over-inked (which is easy do), excess ink can be soaked up with paper towels. One ay to avoid over-inking is to use a timer that will utomatically shut off the motor of the reinker when the peration is complete. Perhaps the most popular of the einkers is the Macinker, a universal reinker which is ompatible with many types of ribbons. The MK/II Inker is lso available for $54.94 (BullPenn Products).

Bede Tech sells a reinker for the Epson brand of rinter ($52.95) and the Imagewriter I and II ($49.00).

Important: Check carefully to make certain you get the ight reinker for the printer.

Card Stock, Labels, and Printers.

rule that contradicts the traditional image of a computer

user gleefully printing out hundreds of labels from
mailing list, is the one that says we should not use labe
in a printer. The reason is simple; labels tend to catch an
stick beneath the platen, and unless you are willing t
spend an hour or two taking your printer apart, you wi
have a large repair bill. Unless you can find labels that ar
guaranteed not to peel off during the printing process, c
own a special "bottom feed" printer, forget it!

A problem that has been nearly universal is that of th
Imagewriter Printer and the thickness and type of catalo
card stock. Some printers simply won't take card stock a
all. The Imagewriter has a tractor feed, but will accep
only rather thin card stock. The problem is "drag" c
friction as paper goes through the printer, causing the car
stock to lose a line every so many cards. By the time th
last card has been reached, the heading may be at th
bottom of the card. A second problem is "microfine
perforations. These look great, since the finished car
looks just like a normal, noncomputer catalog card with n
discernable perforations. However, these same perforation
may peel off too easily. The best type of printer is on
that has "bottom feed" of paper.

Several good vendors for this type of material exis
Some will send a kit of various samples of card stock.

Brodart
1609 Memorial Avenue
Williamsport, PA 17705
800-233-8467; 800-692-6211 (PA)

Follett Software Co.
4506 Northwest Highway
Crystal Lake, IL 60014
815-455-1100; 800-435-6170

Gaylord Bros. Inc.
Box 4901
Syracuse, NY 13221
800-448-6160

Highsmith
Box 800
W5527 Hwy 106
Ft. Atkinson, WI 53538
800-558-2110

The Library Store
Box 964
112 E. South Street
Tremont, IL 61568
309-925-5571

Doing Things Your Way

One thing that the IBM does not have is "friendly architecture." It is difficult for the average user to get inside the IBM and do much in the way of changes. The Apple II on the other hand lends itself to changes. The slots in the back (on the mother board) of the Apple easily accept any of hundreds of peripheral cards on the market. An avid Apple user should never be afraid of opening the Apple and making whatever changes are necessary. Some cautions are advised, however, especially for first-timers. Never use your fingers to pull chips. The proper instrument is an IC puller. They cost just a few cents, and can be obtained from your local vendor. If one is not available, use a small screwdriver or other properly shaped instrument to gently pull one end of the chip up and then the other. Circuit boards should never be yanked or pulled too hard, and pressure should be applied evenly. Make certain when installing a circuit board that it is being pushed into the slot on the mother board properly. Always work with the Apple turned off and unplugged (remove the cord from the back of the Apple). Perhaps the most common injury to a disk drive occurs when the cable is not connected properly over both sets of pins on the circuit board; the board will short-circuit and a chip on the board will burnout. You will be treated to the dreadful aroma of burning silicon. Be careful, such accidents even happen to pros.

An Apple computer will break down just like any othe appliance. A book for helping to solve some of the typica or routine repair problems is Gene B. Williams' *How Repair and Maintain Your Apple Computer* (Chilton, Radno PA, 1984).

Progress is Not Always Progress

After the IIe arrived, Apple decided to "enhance" th machine in order to make it completely compatible with i IIc, the new portable. Whatever advantages this may hav for Apple's marketing team, it has proven to be a proble for many people who are looking to run their software o a second Apple. While your software will most probabl work on a new Apple IIe, you cannot count on it. On source of the trouble might be this "enhancement." Thi can be solved, however. A product called *Switchbac* (Computer Accents, Inc., $59.95) makes it possible t "de-enhance" your machine whenever you want.

DOS vs. ProDOS

It is important that Apple owners understand th difference between the two major Apple operatin systems, DOS 3.3 and ProDOS. DOS was the firs operating system available for the Apple; ProDOS is latecomer. For most small applications, DOS is just fin Unfortunately, if you are working with a large hard dis with many megabytes of storage space, it can becom difficult to manage effectively with the file handlin provided by DOS. ProDOS will handle more file name per volume and will subdivide each large hard disk int subvolumes or directories.

When To Computerize and When To Not

A word processor is going to be the program most usefu to nearly any library, and while it cannot replace th typewriter completely, it can relieve us of much of the dul routine typing tasks that we are used to, as well as spee

p the production of memos, letters, etc. Larger libraries
systems often have available mini or even mainframe
)mputer systems. These systems may be more efficient for
ose who can afford them, but they are beyond the reach
smaller libraries.

This is a good point at which to discuss the myth that
/erything can be or is worth computerizing. Nothing could
e further from the truth. Typing a single card or address
bel is typewriter work. Similarly, a list that is only of
oderate length and requires nothing more than simple
iphabetization, can be sorted by hand and typed out.
)metimes, a card file works best. I have seen librarians
ruggling with sophisticated micro database systems just to
repare a list of names and addresses of twenty records.

At Maywood, I use a word processor to prepare
oilerplate (text that is used over and over again) of Board
iinutes, the monthly report outline (I fill in the month's
/ents at the headings), and for various other similar
isks.   If I have an envelope to address, I use the
/pewriter which sits beside my Apple. (I also have my
pple connected to a modem and telephone so I can work
n Lincolnet, an electronic bulletin board system for the
ublic, without ever leaving my office.)

A Personal Note

eople (most often salespeople, but others, too) will
onstantly try to get their friends to update and move on
） the "latest" thing. Though I have recently been using
ppleWriter IIe for certain applications, I have been an
vid user of *PieWriter* for the past six years, which I still
elieve to be the best word processor ever made for the
.pple. Unfortunately, it has been discontinued by Hayden.
he point is: if your machine and software do what you
eed them to do, then don't change unless you can think
f a good reason. Sometimes, better products arise that do
hings that are better and handier. For instance, *PieWriter*
/ould never hold large documents (over 3000 words), which
; a problem, though I have long since found easy ways to
et around it. Changing software, even for good reasons,

requires an investment in time, especially if it is a wor
processor, spreadsheet, database manager, or othe
sophisticated programs.

Where To Put It?

If your desk area is not sufficiently isolated to prevent th
curious from playing with your machine, there are lots o
devices for locking it up or bolting it down. One popula
cabinet is manufactured by Bretford. It provides amp
space for most normal peripherals, including hard drive
printers, monitors, and can be locked up when not in us
It will not stop anyone with a crowbar, but then very litt
will.

References

1. Information taken from the R.R. Bowker Company
"National Library Microcomputer Usage Study 1984."

2. Information taken from the July 1985 statistic
analysis of the PLA Library Microcomputer Users Databas

MAJOR SOFTWARE 1:
APPLEWORKS

hough strongly beaten by many single-function packages, *ppleWorks*, as a whole, is quite excellent, especially for **e** person with moderate or intermediate needs. *ppleWorks* combines the three most common software usiness capabilities that exist--word processing, spread-**eet**, database manager--and it's also easy to learn!

What doesn't *AppleWorks* have? There are a few **ings**. These include telecommunications (the ability to **n**port or export data over the phone lines without exiting **a** terminal program), and graphics such as charts and **i**agrams that are meant to emphasize some point in a ocument. Such charts can still be used, but they must be **a**de with another program, and then "cut and pasted" into **e** report (or made a separate page which will obviate the **e**ed to paste anything onto another page).

AppleWorks cannot live up to the expectations of **'**ordPerfect, but it can be recommended on the basis of **e**velopment and experience. Librarians in great numbers **a**ve been pushing it to the limits for some time to prepare **s**ts, magazine control, acquisitions, statistics, and most **'**ord processing functions (memos, letters, reports, and **v**en manuals). The documents and forms created with each **f** the *AppleWorks* modules can be switched back and forth **e**tween each by using the desktop function which will **l**low up to twelve different (but still separate) documents **a** memory at one time.

AppleWorks can be easily divided into three **o**mponents: the desktop, the clipboard (buffer), and the **i**le management system. From the desktop, you can go **n**ywhere: edit a file, load or save a file, format, etc. Just **k**e the traditional desktop we all work with on the job, **h**e computer desktop contains all of the materials or areas **f** work we need, ready for our selection and use.

The *AppleWorks* Desktop looks like this:

Disk: Drive 1 MAIN MENU

Main Menu

1. Add files to the Desktop
2. Work with one of the files on the Desktop
3. Save Desktop files to disk
4. Remove files from the Desktop
5. Other Activities
6. Quit

As you can see, *AppleWorks* is a menu-driven progra. Nearly all commands can be obtained simply by pressing number from a selection displayed on the screen. This sam principle works with the editing mode as well. By typin the control-closed-Apple sequence, a help screen appea which will give information on cursor control, moving tex and other commands.

The Clipboard is the integrating element of the syster By transferring parts of files from any component to th Clipboard, they may be moved into any other componen So, if you have a statistical table that you made using th spreadsheet, it is simple enough to move it to th Clipboard, and then back again into the word processor have as part of your report.

Use in Libraries

Acquisitions work has been reported at the Brunswick Glynn County Regional Library using the databas component. Using an extended memory card, RAMwork and the Apple hard drive, Profile, the computer syste replaces an earlier paper file, each record corresponding t one of the paper forms. In addition to replacing the ol stem, new functions have resulted as a by-product. For stance, using a word processor to produce catalog cards as resulted in notebooks of copies of all cards of books rocessed within the past few years, saving staff time arching for the material elsewhere. A more extended say of this topic is contained in a long article in *Apple ibrary Users Group Newsletter* (April 1986).

Circulation statistics work has been reported at the rban Campus Library of the Des Moines Area Community ollege using the spreadsheet portion. The library created veral forms, then used the formula building capabilities compute percent of increase/decrease in circulation, verage daily attendance, collection records by LC assifications, etc. In particular, it was said that *ppleWorks* was preferred because it was possible to move e spreadsheet work directly to the word processor ithout changing programs or using real cut and paste.

Periodicals management was performed at the Merivale ranch of Nepean Public Library in Ontario, Canada, to ontrol 452 titles and 438 active subscriptions. The atabase section was used to categorize each periodical tle by type (where it belonged) as well as collection eference or circulating), language (English or French), nd source of the subscription.

Add-on Programs

opularity brings with it all sorts of advantages, but most nportantly it means manufacturers have and will continue develop related products such as templates and tutorials nat will integrate with *AppleWorks*.

Graphics Add-ons

raphWorks

raphWorks (PBI Software) is a graphics package pecifically designed for use with *AppleWorks*. Using data

directly from the *AppleWorks* spreadsheet, this program w
create pie, line, bar, and stacked bar graphs. It will al
print spreadsheets that are too wide to fit on a norm:
page, "sideways," down the page. $79.95.

Telecommunications Add-on

Point to Point

Point to Point (Pinpoint) is a telecommunications softwa:
package that offers binary or text file transfer (Xmoden
and up to 2400 baud using *AppleWorks* filecard interfac
Files may be sent or received unattended, if desired, usir
a clock card. So, even in telecommunications, the migh
Apple II has an answer. $129.

CommWorks

CommWorks (PBI) is another communications progra
specifically designed to integrate with ProDOS an
AppleWorks, and contains macros, file-folder interface, a
online text editor, autolog facility, and supports the Haye
2400-baud modem and the new 3.5-inch UniDisk, as well :
many RAM expansion cards. $95.

MailMerge

InfoMerge

InfoMerge (Pinpoint) is an easy way to obtain mailmerg
capability using *AppleWorks*. Interfacing with both th
database manager and the word processing progran
InfoMerge allows for an on-screen, direct-print mailmerg
package. $79.

Desktop Accessories

eves

eves (PBI Software) is a desktop program that can be ed with or without *AppleWorks*. To invoke *Jeeves*, simply press the Apple keys on each side of the spacebar. The *eves* startup menu then comes into view:

Jeeves

Getting Started

1. Load another program with Jeeves standing by
2. Printer: Printer Port
3. Modem: Modem Port
4. Path: /Jeeves/
5. Take the day off

Jeeves provides for a calculator, schedule (appointment lendar), alarm clock, phone book, a note pad, and special rsor and editing keys. A short booklet describes how to stall and use the system, but users should be cautioned at *Jeeves* will only work with a special hardware nfiguration, which includes an Apple IIe with 128K, and 1 interrupting source (either an AppleMouse IIe, a hunderclock, a ProClock, a Timemaster II H.Q., or a PBI terrupt board). *Jeeves* will work with nearly all plications, not just *AppleWorks*, so it has a wide range ' utility. It does take up RAM space, so you will lose me document size which should only be noticeable to ers working on large documents with very limited (128K ' under) RAM space. $49.95.

Fingertips

Fingertips provides users of *AppleWorks* (as well as oth
programs) with a program that is compatible with mo
Apple IIs (including II and II+), ProDOS or DOS 3.3, ar
forty- or eighty-column display. Some of its featur
include: four function calculator, hex calculator, scientif
functions (Sin, Log, etc.), telecommunications (send
receive files, autodial from directory, terminal mod
database functions such as mailing list filer, printing labe
or lists, calendar/planner, notepad, and printing functio
such as a screen dump. Clearly, this sort of utility cou
replace the Rolodex, phone list, notepad, and other thin
typically found on a desk. *Fingertips* also lets the us
perform all DOS or ProDOS commands from within th
program, without ever leaving the word processor. $39.95.

Fingertips
Main Menu

A. Calculator	F. Planner
B. Calendar	G. DOS
C. Notepad	H. Help
D. Rolodex	I. Display
E. Telecom	J. Quit

Still More Power

MacroWorks

MacroWorks (Beagle Bros.) adds the glossary by itself
with *AppleWriter*. By typing just a single keystroke, use
may insert an entire word or phrase into a documen
eliminating drudgery and a source of errors. It also dress
up *AppleWorks* in other ways, including making the deletic
of text at the cursor easier. In addition, this module wor
with the database manager and the spreadsheet. Any of ter

sed function can be summoned from within the program.
rint format can be improved with *MacroWorks* by making
ossible the printing of columns for newsletter production.
34.95.

Compatible with RamWorks

eportworks, ThinkWorks and Megaworks

eportWorks, ThinkWorks and MegaWorks (all by Megahaus)
re all popular add-on programs, providing significant
ncreases to the power of *AppleWorks*. *ReportWorks* is
erhaps the most important of the three, and is basically
n extension of the spreadsheet. Its use offers a new range
f opportunities to the use of the spreadsheet, including
hirty-five additional math functions, and the ability to
electively pull segments of a spreadsheet for individual
eports. $125.

ThinkWorks is an idea or outline processor. This new
ype of tool is actually an extension of the word processor,
aking it possible to conveniently organize articles and
apers during the planning process. Instead of having to
erform the menial tasks of numbering and indenting, the
rogram does it automatically. It is not a full-fledged word
rocessor by itself, but it does make arranging and
earranging single lines a simple chore. $125.

MegaWorks is a mailmerge and spelling program.
125.00.

pellbound

pellbound (Quorum International, Unltd.) is a spelling
hecker that works only with *AppleWorks* on "suspect"
ords (words that may be misspelled). Since no dictionary
an contain all words, such a program has the most
ommonly used words, rarely proper names such as "John"
r "Smith." Spellbound has a dictionary of only one
housand words (the most frequently misspelled, according

to the publisher) so it does not take much RAM space. I
also has an advantage over many other spelling checkers i
that it may be used during the preparation of a documen
automatically replacing words that are misspelled. Spellin
checkers make one aware of words that we may think w
can spell but cannot. This can be a real shocker to al
but English teachers. It helps to remove typos from text
something most of us can use help with. Words may b
added or deleted from the dictionary by using th
AppleWorks word processing module. $49.95.

Don't Have a IIe?

You can still convert *AppleWorks* to your II+ with th
assistance of *Plus-Works* (Norwich Data Services Ltd.
Plus-Works goes far beyond this, however, and makes man
additional functions available. These include a greatl
enlarged desktop, a database of up to 4,200 record
support of most major eighty-column cards, ramdisk, an
supports all versions of *AppleWorks*. The program comes i
two versions: *Plus-Works* ($19.95) requires *AppleWorks*
Apple II+, 64K, eighty-column card and shift-ke
modification. The maximum desktop for this version is 10K
Plus-Works-XM ($49.95) requires (in addition) a Legen
Saturn, or compatible RAMcard, Apple memory car
Microtek, Orbital, PCPI & Micropro CP/M, IBS 108 AP3
or Apple IIe with RAMcard.

Templates

Among the many templates available for *AppleWorks* ther
is an entire set by the Q-Mar group. These cove
encyclopedia disks that make many document disks availabl
as learning aids (Monroe Doctrine, Declaration), recip
disks, general ledger, time management, (schedule, goal
priorities), business letters, contracts, personal financ
graphics/advertising system, homebuilder's tools, teacher
tools, etc. These modules are priced from $9.95 to $89.9
(since this is a subscription series, prices are somewha
less for subscribers).

ibraryWorks

ibraryWorks is a set of templates, especially designed for se by librarians. The accompanying booklet is a ep-by-step description of the templates on the disk. The emplates now make it possible to do mailing lists, eriodical checking and training, catalog card production, cquisitions tracking, statistics, bibliographies, and udgeting and forecasting without a whole lot of user fort. $26.95 (plus $2 shipping) prepaid.

Tutorial

ppleWorks Simplified

ere is one method for those who think that they may eed some additional help with *AppleWorks*, a simple itorial approach. *AppleWorks Simplified* (Software implified) is a fourteen lesson set of seven tapes and ardboard keyboard overlays. $175.00. Lessons include liting, printing, creating lessons and memos, creating eports, database, spreadsheet, cut and paste, converting les, problem solving. Excellent software for the person ho wants a specialized personal tutorial on most of the sentials of this program.

Bibliography: AppleWorks

ob Ericson has written a book which is particular note-orthy for librarians, entitled *Notes for AppleWorks* ybex). *AppleWorks* has never been known for its ocumentation, so this book fills in the gaps with a ollection of notes about the program based on firsthand perience. For more information, write Mr. Ericson at Box 5064, Rumford, RI 02916.

ron, Arthur. *Using AppleWorks*. Que Corp (Indianapolis, IN, 1985).

Bolocan, David. *Advanced AppleWorks.* TAB (Blue Rid₤ Summit, PA, 1986).

Campbell, John. *Working with AppleWorks.* Haydе (Hasbrouck Heights, NJ, 1985).

Ericson, Robert. *AppleWorks: Tips & Techniques.* Sybе (Berkeley, CA, 1986).

Flast, Lauren, and Robert Flast. *AppleWorks Applicatior* Peking/Viking (Berkeley, CA, 1986).

Lein Ho, May. *AppleWorks for Librarians.* Hi Willoı Research & Publishing (Fayetteville, AR, 1986).

Lein Ho, May. *AppleWorks for School Librarians.* I Willow Research & Publishing (Fayetteville, AR, 1986).

Matthews, Carole Boggs. *AppleWorks Made Easy.* McGra Hill, 1985.

Rose, Richard. *AppleWorks User's Handbook.* Webı Systems, Inc. (Cleveland, OH, 1985).

Rubin, Charles. *Command Performance: AppleWorks, tı Microsoft Desktop Dictionary and Cross-Referen Guide.* Microsoft Press/Harper Row (Bellvue, WA, 1986]

Tamm, R.W. *Applying AppleWorks.* Bristen Press, 1986.

Witkin, Ruth K. *Managing with AppleWorks.* SAΝ (Indianapolis, IN, 1985).

MAJOR SOFTWARE 2:
APPLEWRITER

ppleWriter is a word processing program with more power
ıan that provided with *AppleWorks*. The glossary function
f *AppleWriter* is a macro. Macros are another word for
utomatic typing or coding. By defining a keyboard code of
wo keys to stand for a longer or difficult to type term,
sers save a lot of time and improve accuracy. The
ıpen-Apple" combined with any letter or character on the
eyboard will do the job. A code is defined by invoking
ıe Ctrl-G command and then making the code the first
:tter before the definition (e.g., the code for typing in
ncyclopedia would be "eencyclopedia," if you wished to
ave encyclopedia pop out on the screen at the cursor
osition each time the "open=Apple-e" combination is
epressed). The glossary function makes insertion of long
r difficult to spell words or phrases as easy as the touch
f a button. Let's take a phrase such as, "Public Library
*istrict." If you have to type it, say, fifty times in a
ocument, it will save you a lot of time just hitting a
wo-key code than to type out the entire phrase.

The program is menu-driven. The print functions are
ll displayed on the screen, users simply choose from
mong the different print parameters (e.g., print
estination, page number, headers/footers). It is also
ossible to split the screen into two separate portions of
ıe document or two different documents.

From menu commands users may also embed these same
ontrols into the text, creating greater and more selective
ontrol over the document than would otherwise be
ossible. For example, a good attribute of *AppleWriter* is
s ability to display text on the screen as a "what you see
what you get" mode, though this must be handled
eparately. The alphabet soup keyboard commands make the
se of *AppleWriter* easy to learn, since they are generally
.nemonic in nature (e.g., p = print, s = save, etc.).

AppleWriter has an unusual, but efficient buffer fc deleting and/or restoring a word, line, or paragraph of tex with a keystroke. New users will find it awkward the firs time, but once the necessary keystrokes have been learnec it works well.

AppleWriter cursor control is quite good also. The fou directional arrows of the Apple IIe may be used, but mos users will find it far more efficient to use the keyboar control characters of J, I, K, and U. By using th closed-Apple and a directional arrow, the cursor may b shifted up or down twelve lines, or right or left twelv characters.

Document Size

I use *AppleWriter* with 128K RAM which provides fo approximately five thousand words. Not too bad, but larger document may be prepared in smaller sections suc as chapters. With a RAMcard, the amount of words in file should approach book size.

Boiler plate

The greatest efficiency of a word processor is th production of boiler plate. Boiler plate is the reusing o the same paragraph or section of text over and over. Fo example, if you are writing for a request for the third tim this year, but to a different person, you would be able t load the first one back into memory, change the nam address, and pertinent passages, and have the compute retype it as a new letter. Grant requests and similar item can all be done the same way. I have drafted the basi outline of my monthly Board of Director's meeting an saved it to disk. When the time comes, I load the file bac into the computer, and fill in the "blanks" with the nev data for the new month. This is also great for statistic forms that do not require spreadsheet attention.

Tutorials

Instructional Tapes (FlipTrack Learning Systems) covers many of the major software packages available for the Apple, in particular *AppleWriter*. This system has three audio cassette tapes that cover three levels of word processing: getting started, moving ahead, and shifting into high gear. The first covers such simple things as initializing a diskette, their care, booting the system, using a hard disk, cursor control, deleting and retrieving files. The second tape covers moving and retrieving paragraphs, search and replace, tabs, formatting text, print commands, and more. The final tape covers forming glossaries, form feed commands, special commands, complete instructions.

Talk-U-Thru (Adrian Vance) is a set of three cassette tapes (audio) for use with *AppleWriter*. $29.95.

ACCOUNTING

General Accounting

General Accounting (BPI Systems), a ProDOS program, is recommended for small- to medium-size businesses, including libraries. It combines many accounting functions, including general ledger, accounts receivable, accounts payable, cash disbursement, and payroll functions. The system uses five different disks for startup, posting, data entry, and maintenance. A fictitious company's books are also included on a separate disk as part of a tutorial. The system is explained step by step and you should have a general grasp of accounting principles before beginning, if just to smooth the planning and data entry process. $395. 48K Apple II/II+; 64K Apple IIe; two disk drives, printer required.

AV MANAGEMENT

A-V Catalog Writer

A-V Catalog Writer (Follett Software Co.) is an off-the-shelf catalog program for putting up to one thousand audio-visual items on a single disk. Six descriptors are: media type, shelf list number, title, producer, contents and copyright date, and up to three subjects. Three different catalogs may be produced: shelf list by Dewey number, shelf list by media type, and subject catalog. Users may add to, change, or delete any entry at any time. Either the entire catalog or specific subject catalogs may be printed out and distributed. Up to twenty media abbreviations and forty different subjects may be specified for quickness of data entry. $79.

The A-V Handler

The A-V Handler (Media Logic Co.) is an AV scheduling and inventory system. It can also be used as an online media catalog and will allow materials to be booked by the room and hour. Other features include: on-screen and hard-copy reports, rental film/vendor management, and calendar scheduling. This CP/M program requires a CP/M card. $2,500. $50 demo kit.

Disk Catalog System

Disk Catalog System (New Dimensions) is a system for maintaining a catalog for computer programs. **(See Figure 1.)** The system does not read the catalog from the disk, so data must be manually input. Since most program disk catalogs cannot be read anyhow, this is definitely a quick easy way to maintain a printed catalog list without retyping one each time new software arrives. Fields include age level, location, producer, price, Dewey number, curriculum area, disk name, program name, and a description. The system also prints disk labels if desired. The disk catalog itself consists of a printout of each disk's contents (a numerical listing of programs, with location). A

DISK   CATALOG   SYSTEM

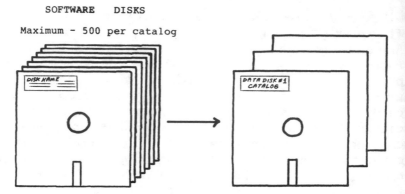

SOFTWARE   DISKS

Maximum - 500 per catalog

The programs stored on each Software Disk are entered and stored as sequencial sets of program records which contain the disk name, seven other common fields, and the program name with its description.

DATA   DISKS

Maximum - 900 program records per disk

OUTPUT

CATALOG
with
Index

SOFTWARE
Disk
Labels

Figure 1.

complete alphabetical listing of programs may be printed out (index), with area, age level and page numbers. Clearly, this is an ideal program for anyone dealing in public-access micros (school or public), or a large staff collection. Manual with full instructions, printouts of actual catalog and index, and menus included. $30.

Photo Recall

Photo Recall (Combase) is a filing and retrieval system for photographic images. Slides or pictures are automatically given a number by the computer as data about them is entered. This number is used for filing. Twelve main categories are available for classification, with 120 classifications within these twelve. Eighty-four of the categories are predetermined, the remainder are entered as desired by the user. The Personal Version allows for the addition of categories, but it does not allow for editing of the predetermined categories, which the other versions do. A printed list of materials in the system may be produced. The program comes with documentation and enough materials for numbering 500 images (labels). It is in use at the Chicago *SunTimes*. $40, Personal Version. $50, School or Professional Version.

The Software Librarian

The Software Librarian (Educational Activities, Inc.) is another in the growing number of software catalog programs. One feature of interest is search capability by title, grade level, and subject, so it acts, in effect, as a small online catalog. The program is easy to use, menu-driven, and comes with a looseleaf binder with complete instructions. $59.95, includes backup diskettes.

Main Menu

Would you like to:
(A) See the directory?
(B) Create a file?
(C) Modify a file?
(D) Search a file?
(E) List a file?
(F) Delete something?

Press the letter of your choice

Video Recordit

Video Recordit (Right On Programs) is an easy system for keeping track of videotapes. Users enter the name of the videotape, the computer then assigns each a consecutive identification number. A list by number or alphabetical by title may be printed. Lost cassettes may be edited out or labelled "lost" in the printout. Output may be to the screen or to printer. $50. Capacity unknown.

BIBLIOGRAPHY PRODUCTION

Bibliography Ver. 1.6

Bibliography Ver. 1.6 (Pro/Tem Software, Inc.) is a specialized bibliography program, different in nature than most of those seen elsewhere. The program works from a user prepared library of bibliographic citations and constructs a bibliography of references in a book, article or other manuscript. Each citation found in the library is automatically added to the bibliography. Keynames help the program to identify each citation in the library. The program will also replace the keynames in the manuscript with the library entry if desired. A separate word processor may be used to create the library or use Pro/Tem's *Notebook*, a database manager. $99.

Personal Bibliography System

The Personal Bibliography System (Personal Bibliographic Software) is the ultimate in bibliographic production, providing several options for users, as well as the ability to change and modify virtually anything. Twenty different document types are "built-in" to the system. **(See Figure 2.)** Simply identify which type of document you are inputing and the system does the rest. $250.

Bibliography Writer

Bibliography Writer (Follett Software Company) will produce professional quality bibliographies with a minimum of effort. Bibliographies may be stored seven to a disk and contain author, title, call number, city, publisher, copyright, and an annotation. Unlike the *Personal Bibliography System* listed above, this program cannot be easily customized or modified for specific use. $59.95.

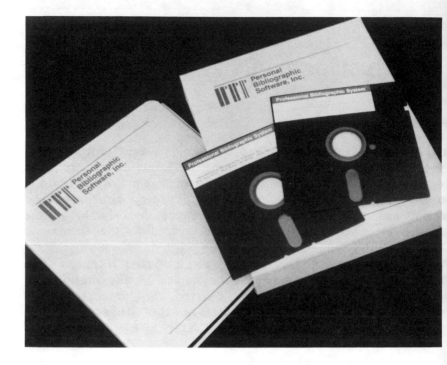

Figure 2.

BLIND AND PHYSICALLY HANDICAPPED

Libraries can now offer computerized services for the blind or handicapped. The basic problem is how to enter information into the computer and get the results out again--in a format that can be understood by a blind or deaf person. Most of us are familiar with the Kurzwiel reading machine, but in recent years, with the advance of technology, a wide range of new equipment and software has become available that will do everything from read text from a book or screen, to creating braille via special membranes attached to a computer. Some of the developments involve software that is now available for the Apple. The Phoenix Public Library has taken a step ahead with its newly created Special Needs Center (see reference below).

Artic Vison and Artic Screen Reader

While there are many forms of special devices and software, we are only going to look at one produced by Artic Technologies, *SynPhonix*, which is actually two products for the Apple II Computers. (See **Figures 3 and 4.**) The first is an electronic speech articulator or hardware component (SynPhonix 100) to produce excellent sound, the second is the *Artic Screen Reader*, a software component that translates the screen or keyboard output into verbal sounds. The system allows user control of sixty-four different speech sounds (phonemes), pitch, loudness, rate, and filter frequency level. Users may program the system in BASIC. Different "lexicons" or groups of vocabulary words, are edited and then saved to disk and retrieved when needed. Some lexicons are preprogrammed and available for purchase (general vocabulary, business vocabulary, computer vocabulary, first names, states, capitals, countries; any two $49.95). The standard package for the Apple includes internal speaker, phonetic speech editor, BASIC demo & text-to-speech, $155. *The Artic*

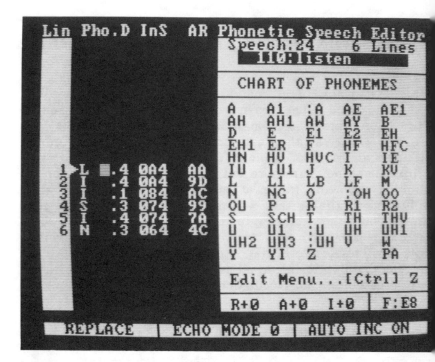

Figures 3 and 4.

reen Reader package includes the standard package mponents plus the screen reader, $250. DOS 3.3 required d 64K.

aster Talker

aster Talker (SEI) is a "pre-boot" program, loaded into e computer prior to the actual running of other programs imilar to the loading of DOS). Once loaded, virtually any EI software will "talk." Specifically designed for the sually impaired, the product may be adjusted for ster/slower, louder/quieter, and may be switched between tter or spelling mode and pronunciation mode. There are rrently over sixty SEI programs that will work with aster Talker, including SAT series, math series, literature ries forcign language series, history and government ries, biology series, and chemistry series. $40.

icro-Interpreter II

icro-Interpreter II (Microtech Consulting Company) is a ogram for teaching signing. More than 2,100 words can signed on the screen by an animated charater. The enu-driven program can speed up or slow down animated otion, and allows for the creation of a file of up to venty-five words. Motions may be "frozen." Signed words e stored on fifteen different disks, but if adapted to a rd drive, changing diskettes is eliminated. Word groups clude: communication, education/occupation, emotion/ eling, family/relative/people, food/nutrition, home/ othing, health/recreation, verbs, locations/travel/ coun- ies/cities, mental actions, religion, various parts of eech, etc. $495, includes master disk and fifteen data sks.

urther Reading

Bowe, Frank G. *Personal Computers & Special Needs.* bex (Berkeley, CA, 1984).

Goodrich, Gregory L. "Applications of Microcompute by Visually Impaired Persons," *Journal of Visual Impairme and Blindness*, V. 78, November 1984, p. 408.

Hooker, Fran. "Computerized Braille: The Bould Story," *Wilson Library Bulletin*, V. 59, April 1985, p. 527.

Roatch, Mary. "Electronic Access to Print Informatic for Blind and Visually Impaired Persons in the Publ Library," *Public Computing*, September/October 1986, p. 3

CATALOGING/ACQUISITIONS

atalog Card Production

' you intend to print catalog cards, you might wish to nsider getting a printer with "bottom feed." This sort of rangement makes it easy for the cards to go through the rinter without getting stuck or "dragging."

vant Cards

vant Cards (Addison Public Library) is a good choice, specially since it was produced by a public library. It is a enu-driven package with over a dozen functions, including bel printing. **(See Figure 5.)** Data entry can be free-form ersions or structured. A proof sheet of data can be rinted out for error checking. The system uses AACR2 unctuation, and includes up to eight subject headings and ight added entries. Cards may be saved for later batch rinting. Data entry errors are easily corrected. Fields are ariable length, with up to 255 characters each (most atalog card programs have fixed length fields that waste ace or force truncated entries). Apple IIe/+ (II+ requires wercase and eighty-column card preferred). $250.

ardprep

ardprep (Learning Technologies and Libraries) has most of e features anyone would expect from this type of rogram. It uses AACRII rules and punctuation, and will rint second or third cards on request, and up to six of ach subject, added entry, and requester cards; complete ard may be displayed on screen before printing; **(See igures 6 and 7.)** all information is saved on disk; fields clude five or eight (optional) call-number fields, content otes, vendor field, optional second-notes field, and utomatic tracing for main entry; optional printing of price

```
R
011              Public library catalog ... supplement to the
PUB                 eighth edition, 1983 / edited by John
                    Greenfieldt and Brenda Smith. -- [Pbk. ed.].
                    -- New York : Wilson, 1985-
                       v. ; 26 cm.

                    LCCN 84-3508.
                    ISBN 0-8242-0702-5.

                    1. Bibliography--Best books.  2. Catalogs,
                 classified (Dewey Decimal).  3. Public
                 libraries.  I. H.W. Wilson Company.  II.


6/21/85 em


R                   BIBLIOGRAPHY--BEST BOOKS
011              Public library catalog ... supplement to the
PUB                 eighth edition, 1983 / edited by John
                    Greenfieldt and Brenda Smith. -- [Pbk. ed.].
                    -- New York : Wilson, 1985-
                       v. ; 26 cm.
```

Figure 5 shows a sampling of Avant Cards.

on labels; adjusts left margin for any printer; ten or twelv
pitch printing; a single replacement card may be printe
without reprinting the entire file; and proof sheet may b
printed to check accuracy of information before printin
cards.

An additional program is required to print labe
(inquire). Detailed documentation with menus leads use
through every step. IIc/e or II+ (with lowercase adapte
chip), 48K. $99.95.

Card-Cat

Card-Cat (Compu-Tations, Inc.) is a menu-driven, prede-ined catalog card program, with batch printing of up to 60 cards (per disk). Fields include: call number, author or main entry, title, media type, subtitle, credit line(s), ublisher, copyright date, pagination, series or set, ontents, notes, subjects, tracing numbers, etc. While the ard data is preset, the card size is not, allowing users to elect for different size cards or forms. Similar cards may e created using defaults, saving time. Will support most rinters. $59.95.

System Menu   Card-Cat
>Load/Change Data Disk<

Add Card(s)
Edit Card(s)
Delete Card(s)
Undelete Card(s)

Print Card(s)
System Maintenance
Configure System
Point to Option and Accept

DelMar Software Card Catalog

DelMar Software Card Catalog (Delmar Software) will print uthor card, title card, four subject cards, and two added-ntry cards. Label production is supported for spine, book ocket, and card. The program has a lot of flexibility when rinting out single or multiple cards or labels. A correction eature and a quit function permit user to easily correct vork or to save it for later session. A proof sheet may be rinted. IIe/+. $125.

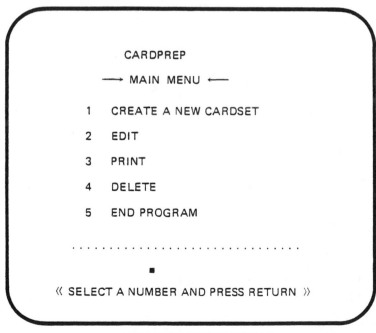

FIRST CREATE SCREEN DISPLAY

MAIN MENU SCREEN DISPLAY

Figures 6 and 7.

ibrarian's Helper

ibrarian's Helper (Scarecrow Press) is a longtime favorite
* mine. It is completely menu-driven with two basic
:ograms: a configuration program and the card writing
:ogram. The system allows for complete customization; if
₁ere are fields that are not used by a library, they may
: deleted from the process, and it is possible to configure
copy of the program for separate types of media (e.g.,
:cords, etc.). Apple II (with CP/M card). $325 (includes
P/M card).

he LPS Catalog Card Program

he LPS Catalog Card Program (Library Processes System)
₁ndles 660 items per disk. The system produces full sets
' cards, or an individual card (shelf list, author, title, one
₁ five subjects, series). It will also produce book lists for
₁ventory, subject lists and new books from the informa-
on. Entries may be deleted, sorted (fiction alphabetically
y title), and even permits subject searches by key word or
·oups of call numbers anywhere on the card. Also included
a spine/pocket/card label programs. This module will
₁clude the following: type (if used), class number, author
tters (cutters), volume/copy number, and, in addition,
ɔcket and card labels include author, title, and biography
f biography). Labels are printed in all caps. Data is taken
₁rectly from entries stored on disk from the catalog card
:ogram. The menu includes the following selections:

1. Labels for individual entries;
2. Labels for a range of entries;
3. Labels for all unmarked entries;
4. Mark/Unmark a disk of entries; and,
5. Generalized label production.

Official OCLC continuous pin-fed, pressure-sensitive
₁cked labels are required (available through The Highsmith
ɔ., Inc.). $225.

Telemarc III

Telemarc III (Gaylord) will print catalog card sets ar labels for book card, book pocket, and spine. This syste (according to the publisher) uses modified Library (Congress MARC tags to receive and store catalogir information for each item. Cards appear on the screen ; they will appear when printed out. Fields are: accessic number, author, title, title proper, remainder of titl author/edition statement, media type, publisher, dat physical description, series note, general note, subje headings, annotation, subject headings, author-added entr title-added entry, series tracing, classification prefi Dewey Classification, LC Classification, author identifie ISBN, LC Card Number, purchase order number/date, co of item, and status. Batch printing is available to spee data entry and printing. This program seems to hav everything, but, even so, one thing going against it f(small libraries is its big price tag, which in some cases, several times that of competing packages. $495. Requir two disk drives, Apple II+/e. Lowercase adapter with II Will work with Epson, IDS, Okidata, and most othe printers.

MENU

1) Check Printer Alignment   E) Edit
2) Make a Card   P) Print Card Set
3) Exit a Program   R) Reconstruct Car(
B) Batch Print Cards or Labels
M) Print Main Entry Card Only
S) Print Shelf List Card Only
C) Sort and Print Main Entry Cards

CIRCULATION

irculation Systems Functions

ome of the programs listed below are true circulation
ystems, including integrated systems, others merely
erform a single function such as keeping track of
verdues. One, *Access-list*, helps in analyzing book
irculation trends.

ccess-list

ccess-list (Real Time Computer Services) provides data for
nalyzing book circulation. Books are entered into the
ystem and the computer automatically assigns a number to
hem. Each time the same book is circulated, only this
umber need be entered into the program again. Sample
eports show access number, name, author, call number,
nd the number of times the book has been checked out.
ummary reports show the percent of books in a range
hat were checked out once, twice, three times, etc. A
imple procedure is to keep a tally sheet at the checkout
esk (or any other system that works), and then enter the
ata (numbers) into the system at any time. This not only
elps to determine which areas of the collection are
requently used, but which specific titles warrant
eplacement when lost or damaged. $40.

ook Trak

ook Trak I (Richmond Software Corporation) is a sophis-
icated circulation ProDOS system that will perform order-
g, card and label printing, and serial control. It will
andle up to 80,000, 160,000, or 250,000 items depending
pon if a 10-, 20-, or 30-megabyte hard drive is used.
ichmond also sells hardware (hard drives, clocks, etc.).
850 (includes bar code label printing program). Barwand,
300. Apple IIe only. Write for free demo disk.

Bookworm

Bookworm (J.L. Hammett) is an inexpensive but bare-bone circulation system, intended for small libraries with a sma circulation, limited budget or hardware for computerizatio For these, it will prove an attractive alternative to mor costly systems. Only six fields are used. These ar borrower's name, grade/homeroom, author, due date, an record number. The lack of a light pen or other data entr method, requires that everything must be entered manuall not a system that appeals to everyone or to libraries wit a large circulation. Borrower information must be reentere for each item checked out, and even for a renewa However, the system can be up and running almo instantly, something that does appeal to small libraries. Th maximum number of patron records that the system wi hold is approximately 1,500 per disk. Records may b searched by any field, or borrower and due date, c homeroom and due date. Reports of books overdue may b produced by borrower's name or by record number. $99.

Circulation Management System

Circulation Management System (Orchard Systems) is menu-driven circulation system. This system has a distin advantage over many others offered in that it does n require any bar codes or other collection preparation wor It will, however, only handle very small collections with si hundred items in circulation at one time. A computer not required during checkout, but only during a brie maintenance period each day. Six hundred items fit ont one disk. If more than six hundred items are in circulatio it is recommended that more than one disk be used, an the borrowers be split into some logical categories betwee disks. Other features of this system include automatic fin assessment (including fine categories and maximum fines overdue slip and list printouts, and title search. One dis drive, and printer capable of 132 columns required. Appl II+/e, DOS 3.3. $150. Demo and manual: $15.

Circulation Plus

Circulation Plus (Follett Software Co.) is a hard disk circulation system that will handle up to 8,000 (30,000 books) patrons on five megabytes, 15,000 (65,000 books) on ten megabytes. The system requires a maximum of five seconds to reach any entry during circulation. Since it is a bar-code system, all books and materials may be coded before the system is up and running, or they may be entered one at a time as materials are checked out. The system has a lot going for it, including the printing of many of the forms associated with circulation (e.g., overdue notices). It also contains its own backup system using the floppy disk drives. Eighty-column printer required, two floppy drives, eighty-column card, five- or ten-megabyte Profile hard drive. $695 ($945 with scanner).

Circulation Plus Main Menu

1. Check Out/Renew Books
2. Check In Books
3. Add/Update Options
4. Print/Display Options
5. System Setup Options
6. Inventory Options
7. Backup/Quit

Enter Option #

Circulation System

Circulation System (MSC Management Systems Corporation) is a single-station system with check in/check out, report generation, searching, overdue notices, variable loan period, grace period, institution code, and backup to floppy disk at the end of each day. $1,500. 64K required. Will also use a hard disk and a light pen.

Computer CAT

Computer CAT (Winnebago Software Company) is a computer version of the card catalog and gives access to holdings by subject, author and title. (See **Figure 8.**) The hardware required is an Apple II+/e with 64K, and two floppy drives, eighty-column card, printer, Corvus hard disk system. The system will find a title in less than two seconds. It is set up by entering the library's holdings into a fill-in-the-blank form. This would seem ideal for certain small high school or elementary libraries, though potential purchasers should keep in mind that, if this is the sole access to library materials, only one student can look up material at any time on each terminal. If a library has space (and money) for a sufficient number of Apples to devote to a micro-based card catalog, the advantages of computerization can be enormous. On the other side, being

MAIN MENU PROGRAMS

The Main Menu has two utility programs which appear on all the menus but are explained in this section. The other menus are all accessed from this point and the Search Catalog is found here.

MAIN MENU

1.   Search Catalog
2.   Master Statistics
3.   Unlock Files
4.   Transfer Data from Floppy
5.   Index 'Selector' Menu
6.   Utility Menu
7.   File Maintenance Menu
8.   Printer Ready ?   Yes
9.   Exit

   Enter the number

To run a program, press the number of your choice. Options 5 - 7 require a password to access other menus. The password is set initially to **CLEAR**. It can be changed from program on the Utility Menu whenever you wish.

Figure 8.

the mercy of fickle technology can also be a problem. If
e system is down, how do you access the collection? This
 not meant to discourage, but merely to keep things in
:rspective: there must be adequate backup and vendor
.pport to make it work. This system will handle up to
4,000 titles depending upon the length of each record and
e size of the hard disk drive. Up to sixty-three stations
ay be added. $995.

›mputerized Absence-Based Management System

›mputerized Absence-Based Management System (Combasc)
 a miniature circulation system with automatic fine
sessment and that will print overdue slips and lists. The
stem will only track six hundred items at one time. A
arch may be conducted by name, grade, due date, call
mber, or fine. A tally search may also be made, in case
 is necessary to know, for example, the number of
udents with outstanding fines or books. A search may be
ther soft copy (to screen), or hard copy (to printer). This
 a simple name- and title-based system. All data must be
tered manually each time a book is checked out. No bar
ding required. $150. Demo disk with manual: $15.

›mpulog

›mpulog (Embar Information Consultants) is a complete
enu-driven catalog system that runs on any CP/M
uipped Apple (it is a dBase II program). It was designed
 be used by special libraries (one example is the
merican Library Association library where it is employed
 catalog a collection of 1,500 folders of various slides,
otographs, and architectural drawings). Each record in
e system consists of ten fields: call number, title, author,
urce, date, pages, ISBN, subject (up to one hundred
aracters), location, and notes. Both on-screen and printed
ports may be generated using Boolean searches, including
ngle field, multiple or all fields. A shelf list and label
ts may also be generated. Storage depends upon drive
pacity. $695.

Two additional programs are available that compleme
Compulog. To add circulation control to the system, it
necessary to purchase *Compucirc*. For serials check-
function, *Compujlrn* is required.

***** Main Menu *****

** Reports **	** Utilities **
A - Author	1 - New CHICAT database
S - Subject	2 - Update catalog records
T - Title	3 - Create SUBJECT file
P - Publisher	4 - Update INDEX files
C - Shelf List	5 - Add records from floppy
L - Author Authority	to hard disk
M - Subject Authority	
N - Source Authority	
B - Labels	*****
F - Field search	H-help
O - Online search	Q-Quit

Due List

Due List (Poway Unified School District) will track up
1,300 overdue items, and list them by due date, authc
student, or class. It will also produce overdue notices. (S
Figure 9.) The program was developed for use by t}
Meadowbrook Middle School (Poway, California), where it
run on a 48K Apple II+ with two disk drives, though t}
program will work with only one drive. Entries may not }
corrected, except in a separate operation. This is a
unsophisticated, though simple and easy to use databas
This public domain program is available for $5.

```
          MEADOWBROOK MIDDLE SCHOOL LIBRARY
DENT: FURSTENBERG

FOLLOWING BOOK IS OVERDUE. PLEASE BRING IT TO THE LIBRARY AND EITHER TURN IT
OR CHECK IT OUT AGAIN.

HOR: SUNSET     TITLE: MICROWAVE COOK BOOK

     OVERDUE BOOK  -  PLEASE RETURN
EMAN                 DATE DUE 11/23/83
05/84                THIRD NOTICE


          MEADOWBROOK MIDDLE SCHOOL LIBRARY
DENT: FURSTENBERG

FOLLOWING BOOK IS OVERDUE. PLEASE BRING IT TO THE LIBRARY AND EITHER TURN IT
OR CHECK IT OUT AGAIN.

HOR: HOLZ    TITLE: MOBILES YOU CAN MAKE

     OVERDUE BOOK  -  PLEASE RETURN
EMAN                 DATE DUE 11/23/83
05/84                THIRD NOTICE
```

gure 9.

brary Circulation Manager

brary Circulation Manager (K-12 MicroMedia) requires
vo disk drives. The program is best suited to small or
ementary libraries with 2,200 students or less. The
aximum number of diskettes required for 2,200 students is
ve. Maximum number of books per student is six. The
atabase contains the student names, addresses, and
omeroom number until graduation. Other information
aintained by the system is the items taken out, items
newed, fines due, and fines paid. Reports that may be
otained include: (by homeroom or student number)
umber of books outstanding, fines outstanding, and search
or a book. Overdue reports, fine slips, preaddressed letters
 parents, and labels may also be printed. Setup time is
arginal; student information may be entered either one-
y-one or (preferrably) in batches. Unfortunately, each
ook title checked out must be entered each time, since
ere is no provision for a light pen. $240. Preview disk:
25.

Menu of *Library Circulation Manager*:

R E P O R T S   M E N U

A. BKS. & FINES OUTSTANDING (S/N)
B. BKS. & FINES OUTSTANDING (H/R)
C. OVERDUE REPORT (S/N)
D. OVERDUE REPORT (H/R)
E. FINE SLIPS (S/N)
F. FINE SLIPS (H/R)
G. LETTERS (S/N)
H. LETTERS (H/R)
I. FINES OUTSTANDING (S/N)
J. FINES OUTSTANDING (H/R)
K. NUMBER OF BOOKS OUTSTANDING
L. SEARCH FOR A BOOK
M. PRINT LABELS
N. RETURN TO MAIN MENU

Library Helper "Overdues"

Library Helper "Overdues" (Southern MicroSystems) is
menu-driven and easy to operate overdue book manage
Functions include printing and listing overdue notices, fin
notices, sort, search, delete, edit and add records, an
review records. **(See Figure 10.)** Approximately fo
hundred students per disk may be maintained. Apple II/+/
$69.

Librarian List

Librarian List (Andent, Inc.) is a set of nine programs f
keeping track of a small collection of up to 10,000 volume
Many of the capabilities of an integrated system are to b
found in this package, including online transfer of file
The principal function is the book/loan catalog in which
book's author, title, publisher, description/subjec
number, loan date, borrower, and other facts a
maintained. Overdues, catalog cards, and other lists ma
be generated. A separate catalog, the "Journal Catalog
will support cost analysis, subscription lengths, and we

```
LIBRARY/IMC NOTICE        !   LIBRARY/IMC NOTICE        !   LIBRARY/IMC NOTICE
YOUR LIBRARY NAME HERE     !   YOUR LIBRARY NAME HERE     !   YOUR LIBRARY NAME HERE

NAME: ADLER, DARLENE       !   NAME: ADLER, TOM           !   NAME: BECKERJECK, MARK

GRADE:  A                  !   GRADE:  9                  !   GRADE: 10

KEY: R                     !   KEY: PB                    !   KEY: R

CALL#: 123.456ABC          !   CALL#: F SMI               !   CALL#: REFERENCE

TITLE: A TITLE CAN CONTAIN UP  !  TITLE: ALAS, BABYLON    !   TITLE: APPLE REFERENCE MANUAL
       TO 46 CHARACTERS

THE MATERIAL LISTED ABOVE WAS  !  THE MATERIAL LISTED ABOVE WAS  !  THE MATERIAL LISTED ABOVE WAS
DUE ON  FRI 04 22 83.  PLEASE  !  DUE ON  MON 04 18 83.  PLEASE  !  DUE ON  TUE 04 19 83.  PLEASE
RETURN THIS MATERIAL.          !  RETURN THIS MATERIAL.          !  RETURN THIS MATERIAL.
```

Figure 10.

indexes. A "Want List" of title, publisher, or source, requestor, and status may be maintained for book loan requests or interlibrary loan. The program will also maintain a listing of personnel, phone numbers, and employment statistics, and a day-to-day staff work schedule. The program also has word processing capability for preparing letters, labels, overdue notes, manuals, orders and form letters. A mailing list program is built-in, too, for newsletters, or other mailing lists. Finally, the program has a lot of flexibility allowing users to create their own additional database for whatever purpose. DOS 3.3. $150.

Overdue Books

Overdue Books (Right On Programs) is a floppy disk database for the Apple computer that automates the production of an overdue list. Ready-made (off-the-shelf) software is written with a specific purpose in mind, and it will usually do only that specific function. It is easy to use. Entries are typed in one at a time and may be deleted as desired. Fields include: teacher, student, title, author, and due date. Entries may be searched for by any field, and all listings may be displayed either alphabetically by teacher or numerically by date, and either to the screen or as a printout. Approximately 1,000 entries per disk.

Overdue Collector

Overdue Collector (Follett Software Co.) is a compani
program for *The Overdue Writer* and will automatical
transfer, on a regular basis (weekly), all active recor
(unreturned books). These records are all maintained on
single disk, instead of being spreadout or lost. $42.95.

The Overdue Writer

The Overdue Writer (Follett Software Co.) will actual
work without a computer on the premises, so long as o
is available for at least fifteen to sixty minutes each da
It is suggested, however, that circulation over one hundr
per day should have a dedicated computer. After data
entered, the system will generate lists, overdue notic
and bills. $129.95.

The Overnight Writer

The Overnight Writer (Follett Software Co.) is a short lo
period check-out system (one or two days, or overnigh
and works essentially the same as *The Overdue Writ
above. The system will hold 150 short-term checkouts. Da
may be entered when convenient. $42.95.

SuperCat

SuperCat (Zephyr Services) is a small menu-driven catal
program that will also print catalog cards. Up to thr
hundred books may be entered into the system if a ha
disk is available, otherwise thirty books per floppy. Boc
data may be entered, deleted, or edited. Eleven forma
may be used to search, display or print data. Thirte
fields include: author(s), title, call number, subject(
publisher, publication date, acquisition date, and price. T
program may be further customized for specific data ent
for a particular library. Sorting by any field is allowe
$49.

ELECTRONIC BULLETIN BOARDS

Micros now allow a small library to maintain an online database for the benefit of the public or for other librarians, for professional networking. Suffice it to say that there are dozens of software packages available from which to choose (see my recent book, *The Essential Guide to Bulletin Boards*, Meckler Publishing Co., for a full description of each), I will describe only one system here, the *GBBS*, which is the software that I installed and use for Lincolnet, the electronic bulletin board system of the suburban Library System (Illinois). There are many good reasons to use *GBBS*, especially when compared with other software on the market. In four months of use, we have not detected a single bug, except for a few things that should have been put into the documentation, but were not. It is a relatively easy program to use.

Something about Lincolnet

Some librarians may not understand what a BBS is, let alone why a library would set one up. An electronic bulletin board system is essentially an interactive online database. Callers (either the public or other librarians) have access to a variety of services, similar to, but not usually as comprehensive as major online utilities (e.g., they cannot compete with CompuServe or The Source, though they are free or at least very inexpensive). For instance, a local BBS will offer electronic mail to its users, but this usually means only local people will call. On the national information utilities, it is quite easy to carry on an electronic conversation between two parties on the East and West coasts. A BBS may also offer free software (public domain downloads), games (usually an interactive fiction game such as *Adventure*), articles (news, columns, poems, short stories), etc. What is offered, and how well it is presented, depends largely upon the enthusiasm and expertise of the individual sysop (system operator). Some of the problems that such a setup presents include hardware,

software, public relations, and purpose. The justificatic
for a BBS by a library is often the public relations aspec
though some of them are run as professional board
serving to facilitate interlibrary loan. A very few do son
online reference as well. The best advice for anyor
thinking of starting a BBS is to be fluent in bas
computer usage first.

GBBS

GBBS Pro (Micro Data Products) comes in either a ProDC
or DOS 3.3 version. Some of its features include multip
bulletin boards, and security levels. These two features ca
go hand in hand. Security level can be better thought of a
a security "area," since they are not arranged in any so
of hierarchy. For instance, if you wanted to have a BE
for the public, but a private one for librarians (which, i
fact, we do at Lincolnet), you could allow access to th
library BBS only to those people whose security had bee
coded for it. But the reverse could be just as true. *GBB*
allows you to code some thirty areas (bulletin board
downloads, etc.) in this way for each caller. Anothe
wonderful feature of *GBBS* is its ease of remote operatior
Complete operation, including renaming files and other DO
file commands can be performed from home or an
terminal. The upload and download sections are exceptior
ally easy to operate.   An "obscenity filter" is include
GBBS uses its own specialized language, ACOS, the *GBB*
program which is documented line-by-line in the manua
Another factor in BBS operation, and one which I foun
from personal experience, is vendor support. *GBB*
personnel are not only willing to help out, they do so in
friendly and clear manner, something that many "techies
find difficult. $125.

```
Ctrl-S Stop/Start  Spacebar to Exit
**********************************************
*     List of supported commands      *
*---------------------------------------------*
*  <(B)> Goto the Bulletin Boards     *
*---------------------------------------------*
* (R)ead !   E -> Examine your stats  *
* (S)end !   F -> Feedback to Sysop   *
* mail  !    G -> General files menu  *
* --------+  H -> Get detailed help   *
* $ = News   O -> Other BBS numbers *
* I = Info   T -> Terminate session   *
* C = Chat   U -> Get a user listing  *
*---------------------------------------------*
* D -> Define system display parms    *
* P -> Change/Update your password  *
* V -> Vote on your computer equipt   *
* X -> Goto the transfer sub-system   *
**********************************************
```

Command (?=Help):

At the time of this writing, there were fourteen bbboards available on Lincolnet: Lincolnet Town Meeting e main board), the library board (for librarians only), a sop board (private), books, library feedback, and VA elpline.

GRAPHICS

1ere are now so many graphics packages for micro-
mputers that it boggles the mind. Some do very
ecialized things, while others perform a whole range of
eful functions. At Maywood, our graphics are handled by
ır acquisitions department, who enjoy making banners for
rthday parties, announcements, and posters and flyers--
l with graphics packages. This is also a way to get
•uble- duty out of an Apple, since catalog card production
•es not take up but a few hours a day on the machine.

vard Maker

vard Maker (Baudville) is another specialized program for
e creation of certificates of all kinds. If it is National
•ss's Day, the staff can prepare an attractive certificate
at says, "World's Best Boss." These can be used to
courage or reward employees, even if in a whimsical or
n-filled manner. Each certificate may be personalized
ith name of employee or patron. Great for summer
ading club awards. Special pin-feed parchment paper is
ailable, too. Both color and black and white printers
pported: Imagewriter, Epson, ProWriter, Apple Scribe,
imate 20, Apple DMP, C.Itoh, and others. $39.95.

ırd & Party Shop

ırd & Party Shop (Walt Disney) is similar to the other
ckages listed here, but with an important difference--it
the only one with Mickey Mouse and Donald Duck and
her Disney characters! Make greeting cards, nametags,
ace cards and mats, wrapping paper, envelopes, banners,
sters, memos, awards, tickets, and signs. **(See Figure 11.)**
/er one hundred graphics include nineteen Disney
aracters with animated features. A handy graphics card
s all characters listed by number for easy use. The
stem works with a variety of printers: Apple Dot Matrix,

Figure 11.

1agewriter I & II, Apple Scribe, C.Itoh ProWriter 8510,
)son JX-80, RX, FX, LQ-1500, Okidata, Panasonic, and
hers. $39.95.

rtificate Maker

rtificate Maker (Springboard) is a handy and convenient
ay to make different awards and certificates with clever
twork. **(See Figure 12.)** Illustrated in the manual are 220
fferent styles. Just pick the number you wish to use and
en customize the design with your own text, font, and
rder. It is very nearly a one finger program. $49.95.

gure 12.

The Graphics Department

The Graphics Department (Sensible Software) is a comple
graphics program for constructing bar, line, pie, scatte
XY, and area charts or combinations of charts. In additi
to the traditional charts, users may also create their ov
drawings, including merge or reduction of picture section
(See Figures 13 and 14.) A "slide show" of up to thirt
two pictures can be created, subtitled, and view
automatically in a pretimed manner. $124.95.

Mask Parade

Mask Parade (Springboard) is a program which desig
masks and jewelry. The selected or customized product
printed out, then glued onto a heavier cardboard a
finally cut out and worn. Great for library parties, speci
events, reading clubs, etc. $39.95.

The Newsroom

The Newsroom (Springboard) is a newsletter program f
creating double-column illustrated newsletters from scrat
(See Figure 15.) The most fascinating aspect of t
program is the way it "wraps" text around a select
picture. Unfortunately, despite all of its many virtues, on
the heartiest will stick with it since the program
awkward and slow. Also, it is difficult to get much on
page unless a reduced type is used but that also makes
very difficult to read. $49.95. Additional clip-art volun
are available for $29.95 each.

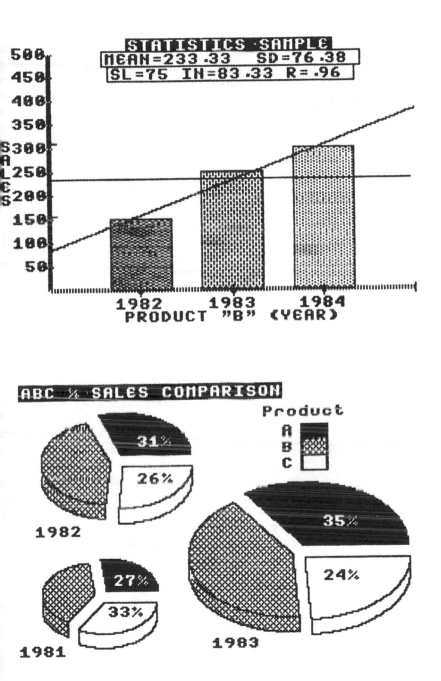

Figures 13 and 14.

THE MAYWOOD
PUBLIC LIBRARY

THE BOOK SHELF

SPRING, 1986 PATRICK R. DEWEY, LIE

This is the newsletter
of the Maywood Public
Library, 121 S. Fifth Ave.,
Maywood, IL 60153.
  Phone: 343-1847 — Main
343-0508 — Branch.

A WORD FROM THE
LIBRARIAN

I thought that I would
share some of the
books which I have read
recently with you. To
my amazement, they
spanned a wide range of
topics, from science
fiction over 80 years
old, to a personal
history 140 years old.

Perhaps the most
intriguing book that I
read recently was The
Vampire LeStat by Anne
Rice. This masterful
work brings the ancient
monsters to life as
never before with
philosophy, history,
beauty and utter terror.

The first in a series,
Princess of Mars by
Edgar Rice Burroughs
was written in 1917. It'
a tale of 12 foot greer
and red Martians. It is
brutal, but a whopping
good story of love and
war on the red planet

SCIENCE FICTION IS
BIG THESE DAYS.

Dandalion Wine, by Ra
Bradbury, is one of th
most nostalgic tales
ever written, filled wit
down-home, country
scenes of Grandma's
cooking, summer
vacation, and the
meaning of mystery fo
a 12-year old child.

Figure 15.

The Professional Sign Maker

The Professional Sign Maker (Sunburst Communications) has as its main function the creation of signs which may be used for report covers, overhead transparencies, banners, and, of course, signs; a few things that *The Print Shop* does not offer are also included. Character spacing, and shading of areas with four levels make the system versatile. Signs may have up to eight lines of text, each seventy-nine characters long. Offers a "save" feature to recall previous work. Works with Apple DMP, Imagewriter, Epson MX-80, Graftrax Plus, ProWriter. $59.

PrintMaster

PrintMaster (Unison World) is the most similar to *Print Shop* of the packages in this section. With this package, one can create greeting cards, signs, stationary, calendars, and banners, using 122 predesigned graphics and patterns, eight type fonts, and eleven borders. (**See Figures 16 and 17.**) The graphics are reproduced in the "User's guide" for quick reference. Anyone using *The Print Shop* (above) will feel perfectly at home with this package, since it operates virtually the same way. One reason for purchasing this along with another such package is the graphics, they are very good and supply you with another source of artwork. In addition, the publisher makes available a number of accessories: color pressure-sensitive address labels, badge kits, disk markers and label pens, and bright colorful packages of computer paper, including envelopes. They also make available the Macinker (inquire and specify printer type; comes with four color sets). $39.95. The *PrintMaster Art Gallery* is a disk of 140 additional graphics for $39.95. *The Creative PrintMaster* by Kendra R. Bonnett is a book of graphic design tips for use with *PrintMaster* available through Unison World for $13.95. It will also work with *The Print Shop, The Newsroom,* and *The Card Shop.*

Figures 16 and 17.

The PrintMaster Art Gallery II

The PrintMaster Art Gallery II is a collection of art work that can be used with either the title program or The Print Shop. Some 140 graphics are included: boom box, school scenes, vehicles, arrows, flags, symbols, etc. As above, the graphics are reproduced in a small booklet for quick identification. $39.95.

The Print Shop

The Print Shop is one of the most seen and glamorous Apple programs around. The secret to its success is twofold: first, it is easy to operate, and second, you get a lot for your return in time, something which cannot be said of very many programs. Figures 18 and 19 are some examples of actual library Print Shop work.

PS Lover's Utility Set

Like AppleWorks, Print Shop now has its own add ons. PS Lover's Utility Set (Big Red Apple Club) offers a set of ten Print Shop utilities, including a graphics capability for print labels and text combined. It also helps to organize graphics better by printing out the picture and name of all graphics on any library disk. $24.95.

School Magic

School Magic (McCarthy-McCormack, Inc.) will produce bookmarks, banners, tickets, awards, permission slips, note pads, invitations, and many other graphics. The pictures have their own style, including a lot that are definitely school oriented (e.g., school bus). $49.95.

Figure 18.

SUN	MON	TUE	WED	THU	FRI	SAT
	1 LABOR DAY LIBRARY CLOSED	2	3	4	5	6 LITERACY WKEND
7 ITERACY WKEND	8	9	10	11	12	13
14	15	16 SLS TERMINAL TROUBLESHOOTING WORKSHOP 8:30 - 12	17	18	19	20
21	22	23	24	25	26 ROSARY COLLEGE "PERSONNEL MANAGEMENT" 9 - 4	27
28	29	30				

Figure 19.

The Toy Shop

The Toy Shop (Broderbund) is an enjoyable way to customize any of twenty working toys and models such as airplanes, carousel, balloon-powered steam engine, sundial, etc. **(See Figure 20.)** The selected project is pulled from the disk, a variety of graphics changes made (patterns, words, etc.), and then printed out. *The Toy Shop* comes with a starter kit of adhesive card stock, wooden dowels, rubber striping, wire, balloons, and cotton cord. Replacement supplies are also available. Each model comes with complete step by step instructions. $59.95. Refill $24.95.

Marvelous Mechanical Models That Really Work

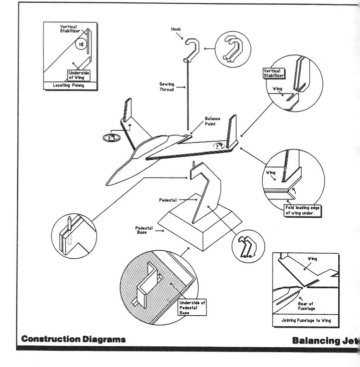

Construction Diagrams   **Balancing Jet**

Build Your Own Balancing Jet Now

Just follow these assembly directions and create your own Balancing Jet, one of the 20 working toys and models included in Brøderbund's new release, The Toy Shop.

Figure 20.

INDEXING

Magazine Indexer

Magazine Indexer is a simple program for keeping track of articles, pictures, or pamphlets, but is also useful for indexing magazines by title of article, magazine, issue, page, two subject headings, and a brief annotation. $75.

INFORMATION AND RETRIEVAL

nformation and retrieval programs and services take many orms, including simple card-file production for reference, nline card files, front-end software packages for online arching, database management systems for all manner of ata storage and retrieval, and reader advisory tasks.

LAnet Plus

LAnet has recently added *ALAnet Plus* (American Library ssociation), a new gateway service that allows users of LAnet to connect with more than seven hundred other atabases without having to subscribe to or learn access rocedures for any but your original ALAnet service. An *LAnet Plus* service retrieves the ten most recent relevant itations for a fee of $8 per search (if the search is nsuccessful, there is no charge). Fees include ALAnet onnect charge, an EasyNet connect charge of $6 per hour, lus the per successful search fee.

Apple Access

pple Access (Apple Computer, Inc.) will turn the Apple II nto an intelligent communications terminal with full apabilities of download, print, and autodial. Files created rith a word processor (letters, etc.) may be transmitted to ther terminals or online systems. Access to online databases, bulletin boards, or any information network is reatly facilitated. Apple compatible modem required. $75.

Byte Into Books

yte Into Books (Calico) is a reader advisory program. fter completing a simple quiz of grade level, gender, nterests, reading ability and enthusiasm, student is natched against a database of five hundred titles already preprogrammed into the system. A printed list of selection gives student titles, authors, shelf location and even a annotation. The program will also report how man students, with grade levels, use the program. Grades 1-: $99.95.

The Great Book Search

The Great Book Search (Grolier) is a game of literature i which students are asked questions from a database of 18 references. The main purpose of this game is to stimulat students to actually read the book. Books may also b searched for by title, author, subject area, main characte and setting. For ages 8-14. $44.99.

The Librarian

The Librarian (K-12 Micromedia) is a simple databas system for keeping track of the predetermined categorie of books, videotapes, magazine articles, programs, records tapes, or recipes. Retrieval may be by keyword o categories, and abstracts of up to 255 characters may b entered for each item. Each library that is created ma contain one or several types of media. A sort by any fiel (except abstract) may be performed and saved to disl Approximately one hundred items (up to five hundred pe disk) may be entered in a single library, making thi program suitable for small quick reference work onl Search results may be printed out. $49.

Library List

Library List (Right On Programs) is a simple bibliograph program for generating lists of new accessions, biographie subjects, etc. The list may be annotated and contain titl author, and subject. $50.

FS: File and Report

FS: File and Report (Software Publishing Corporation) is a
popular set of two software packages that are part of a
larger set of software modules. These two make it easy to
set up or design data-entry forms, sort, and prepare
reports of all types. While they may lack some of the
sophistication of other more powerful packages, they can
be up and running in minutes. The programs do allow users
to make their own backup, however, if the process is done
incorrectly for whatever reason and the backup is lost, and
you will need to contact your local vendor or write the
company directly. About 1,000 records per disk may be
maintained. $125, each.

Base

Base (Applied Software Technology) is specifically
designed to create index card type files. Five diskettes
create records of up to fifty fields each, and a maximum
number of 904 records per file. Reports may contain up to
eight fields each and may be designed according to nine
separate criteria. Records may also be sorted by up to
three fields. Data may be exported to word processors and
other programs to create form letters, and there is also a
built-in mailing list component. A handy, easy to use, and
versatile program for creating ready reference and
community information files is included. $189.

Quick File IIe

Quick File IIe (Apple Computer) is an outstanding menu-
driven database system, with lots of online help. Up to
twenty-six files may be entered on a single disk, fifteen
categories (fields) of twenty characters. Up to six hundred
records will fit in an Apple with 128K. The entire file is
stored in RAM at one time so execution is swift. The
program is very versatile, allowing users to format fields,
widths, record layout. $100.

Reader's Magic Wand

Reader's Magic Wand (Combase), a ready-made or custom
ized database, helps students to find the books they war
with less help from the librarian. Students use th
menu-driven program to indicate their areas of interes
The main menu contains nine different areas (e.g., sport
stories, growing up, etc.). The authoring system (included
allows for titles or subjects to be added or deleted t
match an existing book collection. Users receive a printou
Backup and data disk of popular items included. $75.

Research Manager

The Research Manager (Combase) is a system designed t
file and retrieve bibliographic citations. These may b
books, articles, or any other type of reference. Th
program allows adding, reading, deleting, or printing o
records. A sort program allows users to retrieve a recor
by author, code, or search words, resulting in specialize
bibliographies. While not a standardized bibliograph
program, it will act as a convenient card file for ready
reference or for writers doing research. Apple IIe/c. $75.

Vertical File Resource Diskettes

Vertical File Resource Diskettes (Educational Resource an
Research Service) is a file of information on man
subjects: alcoholism, drugs, abortion, suicide, terrorism, etc
Ten of these sets are available. What these amount to ar
automated vertical file clippings. The articles ar
reproduced along with the ability to search them for ke
terms. A clever and interesting idea for patrons who hav
access to an Apple Computer (or who can use the library'
public access micro!). Each contain about thirty-fiv
articles. The system is a lot simpler than packaging an
checking out pamphlets and clippings, and easier to use
too. A listing of articles is given on volume one (disl
one), with corresponding numbers. If the article is o
another disk, the reader is referred to it. Disk topic
currently available: gun control, homeless/street people i

.S., hunger/poverty in U.S., sexually transmitted iseases/aids, pollution/hazardous waste, teenage pregnancy, 986/7 national debate topics, abortion, alcholism, child buse, diseases, drugs, hi-tech society, suicide, U.S. water olicy, teenagers, family today, women in society, nuclear reeze, terrorism. Each set is contained on two floppy disks r one if the new 3.5-inch disk is requested). ProDOS ersion is shipped, but DOS available by request. $25 per et. $35 per superset.

INTERLIBRARY LOAN

.L Forms Printer

.L Forms Printer (Mack Memorial Health Sciences Library)
his program's principal function is to print continuous-
ed interlibrary loan forms by reading a DIF text file
nerated from a database management system. *ILL Forms
inter* eliminates the manual typing of the ILL form itself
using data which has already been entered into the
tabase. An address file of up to 525 source libraries may
maintained, each accessible by a records number. This
iminates the need to retype the source library address for
request. The database system will also print out an
phabetical list of source libraries with record number, to
d in the adding or deleting of names. Two disk drives
d a tractor feed printer capable of printing twelve
aracters per inch on four-part forms are needed. The
ogram requires the ownership of a separate database
anagement program, such as *DB Master*, capable of
oducing DIF text files. $85. *ILL Forms Printer File*
ontains addresses of health-sciences libraries in
assachusetts and special libraries in Boston area), $25.
B Master interlibrary loan application file used by the
ack Memorial Health Sciences Library at Salem Hospital
equires ownership of *DB Master* to work). All three
odules: $125. First two modules (without Salem
plication): $110.

INVENTORY

veral inventory programs are available that mostly just
ovide an automated listing of many types of materials.
ese may include AV items such as filmstrips, or learning-
supplies, etc.

uip

uip (Addison-Wesley) is a complete inventory system for
V equipment. Printouts by room location, academic
bject, equipment type or manufacturer. Users can
hedule and monitor the use of the equipment; 1,200 items
ay be stored per disk. $165.

hool Inventory

hool Inventory (Educational Courseware) requires two
sk drives and a printer. Capacity is over 1,000 items, an
sy way to maintain an inventory of supplies. Reports may
printed out or viewed on screen. Includes online help
d printed manual. Cost is $50, or $65 with backup.

·

LIBRARY INSTRUCTION

swering Questions Library Style

swering Questions Library Style (Learnco, Inc.) is sically an elementary research skill program, designed to d students to report on essay material in a logical inner. Students may choose from among fine arts, mbols and codes, people of the past, folklore, sports, mous facts, and "then and there." The student is asked to swer a question. To answer, they must determine the key rd and then must look that word up in the card catalog osen from among three cards shown on the screen). The rrect card is finally chosen and a set of high resolution aphics books are displayed with call numbers. Only every her book has a call number and the correct answer is e of the blank ones. This process continues to the index table of contents of the book chosen. In each case, the dent must chose the item that most correctly answers e question or supplies the most information. Appropriate r grade school or early high school. $39.95.

sic Fiction

sic Fiction Skills (Right On Programs) teaches the basic inciples behind shelving fiction books. Fiction, as a ncept is defined then the letters on the spines of the oks are explained. A game using positive reinforcement is ed to test children on the various ideas. $18.

ographies

ographies (Right On Programs) teaches students how to ate biographies on the shelves and provides an planation of why they are arranged in this way, and of e spine markings. A game using positive reinforcement llows. A dozen reproducible activity sheets are also cluded. $18.

Dictionary Skills

Dictionary Skills (Right On Programs) displays dictiona
information as it would appear in print, highlighti
important points with an explanation. A game te
students on the skills that were covered using positi
reinforcement. $18.

Elementary Skills Factory

Elementary Skills Factory (Library Bureau of Investigatic
is similar to Secondary Skills Factory below, but is gear
to grades four through eight. It is not a program that
used directly by the student, but prepares and pri
custom exercise sheets that are divided into elev
sequenced lessons. Material includes Dewey Decimal Syste
locating books, nonfiction, catalog cards, and referen
skills. Before such question sheets can be printed o
there is some preliminary work for the instructor, includi
selecting titles and authors to be in the lessons (the
books actually in the library). A package of cardboard bo
spines and a supply of related materials are included. T
program comes with a useful Teacher's Guide, containing
list of skills/objectives, detailed information on the use
the program, field test report, student activites (includi
a reproducible crossword puzzle), and instructions
editing the program to make the reference book tit
match those actually in the library's collection. Grade lev
4-10. Apple II, 48K. $59.

How Can I find It?

How Can I find It If I Don't Know What I'm Looking F
(Sunburst Communications) is much different than any
the other programs listed here. Its main objective is
introduce students to new reference books and sources
the area in which they are working. Students must alrea
have some skill or experience in working with the ca
catalog, and the locations of books in the library. T
program suggests or recommends specific reference boc
based on what is wanted. For instance, screen one w

quest that the user define a subject area (e.g., people, ces, etc.) **(see Figure 21)**, the second screen will ask for more specific subject (e.g., famous people, ways people e in the United States, etc.). This is continued through veral more screens until a list of suggested reference urces in which to look is presented. The program is easy use and may be customized. New titles that the library tually owns may be added to the list, old ones deleted. oks covered in the program are: encyclopedia, diction-y, almanac, atlas, geographical dictionary, biographical ctionary, index, handbook, directory, yearbook. Includes acher's Guide with suggestions, field test, etc. $59.

gure 21.

w to do Research

w to do Research (Intellectual Software) is an inter-tive tutorial on note-taking, preparing an outline, using e Reader's Guide, bibliographies, card catalog, and mputerized databases. $34.95.

Learning About Catalog Cards

Learning About Catalog Cards (Right On Programs)
excellent for teaching students the fundamentals of t
card catalog. **(See Figure 22.)** They receive explanatio
with illustrations and diagrams of each piece of data: tit
author, publisher, etc. A unit of material is presented, th
becomes interactive, asking students questions (T or
Reproducible master sheets of exercises and examp
included. Librarian's Guide also included. $18.

Learning to Understand the Card Catalog

Learning to Understand the Card Catalog (Right (
Programs) teaches students three different ways of findi
what they need in the card catalog. An introducti
provides basic information, then the program asks a ser
of questions that relate to the correct drawer in the ca
catalog to look. About one dozen reproducible activi
sheets are provided, along with a teacher's guide. $18.

Learning to Use an Index

Learning to Use an Index (Right On Programs) uses a gal
format to teach various principles. The student is "lost
the woods" and only by answering questions correctly c
he or she hope to find the way out. About one doz
reproducible activity sheets are included. $18.

Library and Media Skills

Library and Media Skills (Educational Activities, Inc.) is
three-part program. In part one, students learn about t
use of the guide word in the card catalog, the title pa
and the table of contents. Part two covers the card catal
again, but this time the author, title, and subject cards, '
an, and the" rule of alphabetizing, and encyclopedias. Pa
three covers different types of reference materia
attempting to teach the student how to pick the best o
for a particular need. Covered are the thesaur

RIGHT ON PROGRAMS

THE CATALOG CARD

```
523
ZIM          SUN
             Zim, Herbert.
                 How the sun helps us live by Herbert Zim.
             Morrow. (c) 1985
                 32 p.  illus   color photographs
                 This book tell us all about the sun.  It
             tells why we need the heat and light from the
             sun to live.  It has many photographs.
```

1. What is the name of this book? _____

2. What is the name of the author? _____

3. Put a line under the author's name. It is in two places.

4. In what year was this book written? _____

5. How many pages are in this book? _____

6. Does this book have pictures? _____

7. Are the pictures in color? _____

8. What do we need from the sun to live? _____ and _____

9. What number do we need to know to find this book on the shelf?

_____

10. The number in the corner tells us this is what kind of book?

    Fiction _____

    Non fiction _____

11. Put a square around the number in the corner that tells us where to find this book on the shelf.

igure 22.

ictionary, almanac, book of world records, atlas,
ncyclopedia, book of quotations, and the card catalog. The
et comes packaged in a looseleaf binder with complete
ocumentation. $69.95, includes backup disks.

Library I.Q.

Library I.Q. (Micro Learningware) is a set of five program
that cover library skills at the junior and senior high
college level. *AV Skills* (two parts) teaches the handli
and common maintenance of AV equipment and softwar
definitions and descriptions. Also covered are the Dew
Decimal System, and the card catalog. $50.

Library Search & Solve

Library Search & Solve (K-12 MicroMedia) is an elementar
tutorial in basic library reference tools. The program us
animated graphics and positive reinforcement (high scorer
Hall of Fame), to teach library skills in a puzzle-solvin
manner. $29.95.

Library Adventure

Library Adventure (Learning Well) takes the form of a
elementary adventure game, with rooms, mazes, an
monsters (actually a book worm). Students make their wa
to different rooms in the library (they are assigned a li
of places they must go). When their task is complete, the
make their way to the checkout counter. Amusing gam
apt to keep younger children amused and learning many c
the cut and dry methods. It can be played by up to si
students at one time. Available in two levels: blue lev
(reading level 3.5 to 5.0), and red level (reading level 2
to 3.5). $49.95 each.

Lollipop Dragon

School Library Adventures of the Lollipop Dragon (Societ
for Visual Education) is an exciting multimed
software/filmstrip/tape set for use with elementary scho
children. The complementary parts cover the scho
library, finding what you want in the library, parts of
book, using audiovisual material and equipment. Th
software provides exercises for actual online searching fc

les from a database of one hundred popular children's
les and authors. Reading level of 1.5 to 2.0. Thirty-six
producible skill sheets are included. Complete set: $239;
lmstrips only, $164; software only, $99.

condary Library Skills Factory

condary Library Skills Factory (Library Bureau of
vestigation) is not a program that is used directly by the
udent, but prepares and prints custom exercise sheets
at cover the Reader's Guide, and use the dictionary,
las, encyclopedia and an almanac to answer reference
iestions. **(See Figures 23 and 24.)** Some of the exercises
esent the student with only the title and call number.
udents must then locate specific books on the library's
.elves, either alphabetically or in Dewey order. Before
ich question sheets can be printed out, there is some
eliminary work for the instructor, including selecting
tles and authors to be in the lessons (those which the
brary actually owns). Plastic guidelines that explain the
eader's Guide and other aids are included. There are
ven lessons, forty task sheets in each lesson. $79.95.

ables of Contents

ables of Contents (Right On Programs) uses an actual
ible of contents on the screen. Students answer questions
i order to qualify for a "turn" in a maze. The object is to
:cape the maze by answering the questions correctly. Of
>urse, you must still make the correct turns to get out of
ie maze, even if you have answered all of the questions
>rrectly. About one dozen reproducible activity sheets are
icluded. $18.

'here in the World is Carmen Sandiego?

'here in the World is Carmen Sandiego? (Broderbund) is a
ew twist in learning library skills. Armed with a copy of
ie *World Almanac* and *Book of Facts* (included), you use
our computer and detective skills to learn about thirty

cities and ten possible suspects.　Over 1,000 clues make t
game different each time it is played. $39.95.

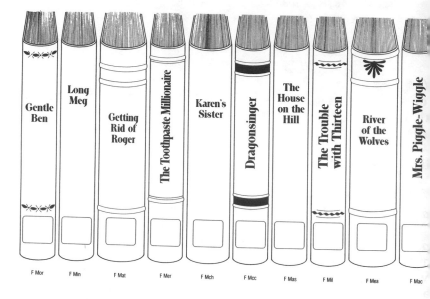

Reference Puzzle No. 1　　　　　　　　Name:_____

ACROSS CLUES

3. The most expensive prison to
operate was built to hold 600 men
but now holds only one.　Who?
5. A mosque is a temple for what
religion?
6. A collie is a kind of dog.　What
kind of animal is a marmoset?

DOWN CLUES

1. In what country does the cahow
bird nest?
2. What river forms most of the
border between Oregon and
Washington?
4. The adjutant is the largest
example of what family of birds

Figures 23 and 24.

MAILING LIST PROGRAMS

Address Book

Address Book (Muse Software) is a menu-driven mailing list program that holds some seven hundred names per disk. Label formatting allows for printing up to six labels across. Data entry is prompted and corrections are permitted prior to saving to disk. The program operates efficiently and with some speed. $49.95.

Mailing List Program

Mailing List Program (Educational Activities, Inc.) is a simple, easy to use program for maintaining a list of up to seven hundred names and addresses. A list or set of labels may be easily printed out. Up to ten separate lists may be stored on a single disk. Any list may be searched for individual entries by name, address, city, state, or zip code. Entries are easily edited and revised. $34.95.

RETROSPECTIVE CONVERSION

itinet

itinet (Information Transform, Inc.) is a system for converting current and retrospective catalog information to a LC MARC format database, which in turn is used to generate MARC tapes and online public-access catalogs. (See **Figure 25**). The program itself consists of two parts: *itinet/retro*, for converting titles on the LC MARC file, and *Mitinet/marc*, for creating original MARC records. union catalogs of Mitinet libraries may also be created.

With *Mitinet/retro*, libraries may begin the conversion process immediately, since it includes LC MARC fiche. Holdings information is accumulated on a floppy disk, then sent to Brodart to be matched with the LC MARC file and create the library's database. $360.

Mitinet/marc is a menu-driven system. Users input one item at a time, as prompted. A MARC record is then created on a floppy or hard disk. $500 for the manual and software.

The interface of *Marchive* and *Mitinet/marc* systems now allows users to receive such services as catalog card production, COM catalog production, and database management. $495.

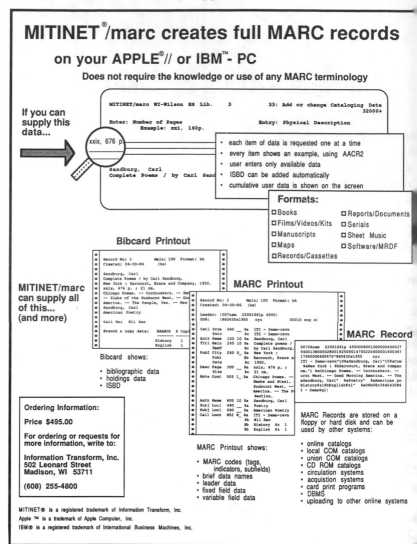

Figure 25.

UTILITIES

...ese help us make copies of files or diskettes, format ...skettes, etc. Usually, those utilities that come with the ...mputer or operating system are bare-bones and rarely ...rk with any speed. Fortunately, there are a number of ...mmercially available packages of considerable quality that ... all of these things (and a whole lot more) with great ...ficiency.

...tcat

...tcat (Beagle Bros.) is a master catalog program with a ...w extras. In addition, to reading DOS or ProDOS files, ...tcat will allow users to sort, search, and print file ...mes. If you want to print out all files that contain the ...tters "WP," *Fatcat* will print out a list. Multicolumn ...talog printouts can also be produced. $34.95.

...S BOSS

...S BOSS (Beagle Bros.) is a longtime favorite of many ...pple computer owners. Its primary function allows users ... change their DOS 3.3 commands. For instance, if you ...n't like to type out "Catalog," all you do is tell *DOS* ...SS to change it to "C" or anything else you want. The ...talog that DOS 3.3 displays may be changed using this ...ility, too. A catalog may contain a new heading, or be ...ore than one column to be able to read it all at once. ...4.

...py II Plus

...py II Plus (Central Point Software) is the best all-around ...ility in existence, especially with the advent of Apple's ...w ProDOS operating system. Files can be transferred ...tween the two systems with impunity, though users of

the Sider hard drives may find some difficulty accessing
second Sider if they have daisy-chained two of the
together. This program is good when backing up
transferring files or diskettes, and will work with a catal
or a subdirectory. For the fastidious person, the progra
will even alphabetize a DOS or ProDOS catalog
directory neatly and quickly.

Copy II+ main menu:

Copy II Plus 6.1
(C) 1982-6 Central Point Software, Inc.

Copy	Sector Editor
Catalog Disk	
Delete	Use arrow keys
Lock/Unlock Files	and return to
Rename Files	select function
Alphabetize Catalog	
Format Disk	
Verify	
View Files	
Disk Map	
Create Subdirectory	
Change Boot Program	
Set Printer Slot	
Quit	Printer
Nov-25-86	OFF

LifeSaver

LifeSaver (Follett Software Co.) is a utility for restorir
data scrambled due to static electricity, magnetic field
and other reasons. The program works admirably, trying
recover any data that remains on the disk. It wi
reconstruct catalogs, partial files, and anything else th
has not been utterly erased. The next time your di:
"bombs," try this program. $35.

onto-DOS

st as there are different programs for the Apple, dif-
rent operating systems have also been developed. One,
onto-DOS (Beagle Bros.), is widely used. With this
stead of DOS 3.3, users may speed up the operation of
eir Apple considerably, to a possible three times. Other
vantages include extra space on a disk (*Pronto-DOS* uses
wer sectors for itself than DOS 3.3), and additional
formation, such as how much free space is on a disk.
9.50.

o-Copy

o-Copy (Micro Data Products) is a ProDOS copy utility.
his product simplifies or makes possible copying files and
lumes, verifying disks, formatting new disks, checking
ive speed, quick disk erasure, alphabetizing volumes
atalogs), viewing files, disk mapping, backup and restore
rd drive volumes, and is completely menu-driven. $39.95.

X

X (Kyan Software, Inc.) is a utility that "pops up" at
cr command with a single keystroke. Displayed in the
X window are many commands that may be used without
aving the program. These include: list, change, delete
rectories, copy, move, or delete files, search for files and
rings, copy, rename, or format volumes, etc. This desktop
stem programs a lot of power and flexibility into the
pple environment. $49.95.

APPENDIX A:

Vendor List

Activision, Inc.
Box 7286
Mountain View, CA 94039
415-960-0410

Addison Public Library
235 N. Kennedy Drive
Addison, IL 60101
312-543-3617

American Library Association
ALAnet Plus
50 East Huron Street
Chicago, IL 60611

Apple Computer, Inc.
20650 Valley Green Drive
Cupertino, CA 95014

Applied Engineering
Box 798
Carrollton, TX 75006
214-241-6060

Applied Software Technology
1350 Dell Avenue
Suite 206
Campbell, CA 95008
408-370-2662

Andent, Inc.
1000 North Avenue
Waukegan, IL 60085

Arktronics Corporation
520 E. Liberty Street
Ann Arbor, MI 49104
313-769-7523

Artic Technologies
1311 N. Main
Clawson, MI 48017
313-435-4222

Baudville
1001 Medical Park Drive S.E.
Grand Rapids, MI 49506
616-957-3036

Beagle Bros. Micro Software
3990 Old Town Avenue
San Diego, CA 92110
619-296-6400

Bede Tech
8327 Clinton Road
Cleveland, OH 44144
800-772-4536

Big Red Apple Club
1105 South 13th Street
Suite 103
Norfolk, NE 68701
402-379-4680

BPI Systems, Inc.
3001 Bee Cave Road
Austin, TX 78746
512-328-5400

Broderbund Software-Direct
Box 12947
San Rafael, CA 94913
415-479-1185

Calico
Box 15916
St. Louis, MO 63114

Central Point Software, Inc.
9700 S.W. Capitol Hwy. #100
Portland, OR 97219
503-244-5782

CMC Computer System
1514 East Edinger #H
Santa Ana, CA 92705
714-835-2462

Coit Valley Computers
14055 Waterfall Way
Dallas, TX 75240
214-234-5047

Combase, Inc.
Suite 890
333 Sibley Street
St. Paul, MN 55101
612-221-0214

Compu-Tations, Inc.
Box 502
Troy, MI 48099
313-689-5059

Computer Accents, Inc.
Box 5905
Kingwood, TX 77325
713-664-9727

Delmar Software
107 N. 4th 5th Street, RR2
Pierceton, IN 46462
219-494-5123

Educational Courseware
3 Nappa Lane
Westport, CT 06880
203-227-1438

Educational Activities, Inc.
Freeport, NY 11520
516-223-4666

Educational Resource and Research Service
Box 66
Barnesville, MN 56514
218-354-7666 or 218-493-4587

Fingertips
830 N. Riverside Drive
Suite 201
Renton, WA 98055
800-628-2828 ext. 544

First Class Peripherals
3579 Highway 50
East Carson City, NV 89701
800-538-1307

Fliptrack Learning Systems
999 Main, Suite 200
Glen Ellyn, IL 60137
312-790-1117

Follett Software Co.
4506 Northwest Highway
Crystal Lake, IL 60014
815-455-1100
800-435-6170

Gaylord Bros., Inc.
Box 4901
Syracuse, NY 13221
800-448-161600

ntellectual Software
98 N. Avenue
Bridgeport, CT 06606
00-232-2224
03-335-0906

Northwest Highway
Crystal Lake, IL 60014
00-435-6170; 815-455-1100 in Illinois

Gray Data Publishing
071 Palmer Square
Chicago, IL   60647
12-278-8080

J.L. Hammett Company
Box 545
Braintree, MA 01284
00-225-5467

Kyan Software, Inc.
Dept. 2, 1850 Union Street, #183
San Francisco, CA 94123
15-626-2080

Learning Technologies and Libraries, Inc
Box 3096
Carbondale, IL 62902
18-529-5723

Learning Well
200 South Service Road
Roslyn Heights, NY 11577
800-645-6564

Learnco, Inc.
128 High Street
Greenland, NH 03840
603-778-0813

Library Bureau of Investigation
1920 Monument Boulevard, Suite 540
Concord, CA 94520

Library Processes System
919 W. Canadian
Vinita, OK 74301
918-256-8598

McCarthy-McCormack, Inc.
1440 Oak Hills Drive
Colorado Springs, CO 80919

Media Logic Co.
757 Creekmont Court
Ventura, CA 93003

Micro Data Products
537 Olathe Street, Unit G
Aurora, CO 80011
303-360-6200

Micro Learningware
Box 162
Amboy, MN 56101
507-647-3705

Microtech Consulting Co.
206 Angie Drive
Box 521
Cedar Falls, IA 50613
800-922-SIGN
319-277-6648 (Alaska, Iowa)

MSC Management Systems Corp.
2155 South 3270 West
Salt Lake City, UT 84119
801-973-5800
c/o John Grey

Muse Software
30 N. Charles Street
Baltimore, MD 21201

Nikrom Technical Products, Inc.
76 Fort Pond Road
Shirley, MA 01464
800-835-2246

PBI Software Inc.
11 Triton Drive, 2nd Floor
Foster City, CA 94404
415-349-8765
800-843-5722
800-572-2746 (CA)

Pinpoint Publishing
Box 13323
Oakland, CA 94661
415-654-3050

Meadowbrook Middle School Library
William Crawford
Pomway, CA 92064

ProAPP
10005 Muirlands, Suite 0
Irvine, CA 92718
800-424-2425

The Public Domain Exchange
2076C Walsh, Suite 511
Santa Clara, CA 95050
408-496-0624

Qmar Group
Box 11215
San Diego, CA 92111
619-455-7513

Quorum International, Unltd.
Industrial Station
800-222-2812

Real Time Computer Services
1706 Bison Drive
Kalispell, MT 59901
406-257-6520

Right On Programs
Box 977
Huntington, NY 11743
516-271-3177

SEI
2360-J
George Washington Highway
Yorktown, VA 23692
804-898-8386

Sensible Software, Inc.
210 S. Woodward, Suite 229
Birmingham, MI 48011
313-258-5566

Sierra On-Line Systems
36575 Mudge Ranch Road
Coarsegold, CA 93614
209-683-6858

Society for Visual Education, Inc.
1345 Diversey Parkway
Chicago, IL 60614
800-621-1900

Software Publishing Corp.
1901 Landings Drive
Mountain View, CA 94043
415-962-8910

outhern MicroSystems
ox 2097
urlington, NC 27216
19-226-7610 or 800-334-5521

pringboard Software, Inc.
808 Creekridge Circle
Iinneapolis, MN 55435

unburst Communications
oom FE 83
9 Washington Avenue
leasantville, NY 10570

ynergistic Software
30 N. Riverside Drive
enton, WA 98055
06-226-3216

Jnison World
150 Shattuck Avenue #902
erkeley, CA 94704
15-848-6666

ephyr Services
900 Murray Avenue
ittsburgh, PA   15217
12-422-6600

APPENDIX B:

Bibliography

Here are just a few of the many hundreds of references of librarians using Apples successfully in their library.

Apple Circulation System," *Small Computers In Libraries*, February 1983, p. 5.

Be C.A.L.M. with your Apple," *Small Computers In Libraries*, March 1984, p. 7.

Boss, Richard W. *Automating Library Acquisitions: Issues and Outlook*, Knowledge Industry Publications, Inc. (White Plains, NY),   1982.

Bunting, L. "How to computerize media management," *Instructional Innovator*, May 1984, p. 39.

Carlin, Don. "Designing a Printed Periodical Holdings List for Your Library Using *dBase II*, a Tutorial," *Library Software Review*, May/June 1986, p. 148.

Computer Cataloging: Quick 'N Easy," *Small Computers In Libraries*. May 1983, p. 3.

Dewey, Patrick. "Follow me to the library: How to make a library bumper sticker or graphics and puzzle software and accessories," *Library Software Review*, May/June, 1986, p. 140.

Kansas uses Apple computer for talking books circulation," *Library Journal*, January 15, 1982, p. 134.

Lundeen, Gerald and Carol Tenopir. "Microcomputer-based library catalog software," *Microcomputers for Information Management*, March, 1983, p. 6.

Printing Catalog Cards," *Small Computers In Libraries*, May 1984, p. 2.

Rains, Nancy. "Designing a bibliography program for a hig school library," *Library Software Review*, May/Jun 1986, p. 152.

"Software Reviews: Catalog card preparation programs, *Apple Library Users Group Newsletter*, September 1984 p. 8.

Sukovich, John E. "Acquisitions with *dBase II*," *Sma Computers In Libraries*, August 1983.

APPENDIX C:

Apple or Library Related Computer Magazines

+
Ziff-Davis Publishing Co.
One Park Avenue
New York, NY 10016. $24.95/yr.

Apple Library Users Group Newsletter
Monica Ertel
Apple Computer Documentation MS 26B
0650 Valley Green Drive
Cupertino, CA 95014
Free

Anyone can find a place in this paper of interest. It
is written by its readers on an informal level to share
their views and ideas (a sort of written users group).

Call A.P.P.L.E.
Apple Puget Sound Program Library Exchange
90 S. W. 43rd Street
Renton, WA 98055
206-251-5222
21/yr

CMC News
15 Oak Street North
Cannon Falls, MN 55009
507-263-3711
9/yr prepaid

incider
Box 911
Farmingdale, NY 11737
24.97/yr

Hot Off The Computer
Westchester Plaza, CWEP
Elmsford, NY 10523
20/yr

Library Computing is a semiannual section of *Librar*
    Journal.
Box 1977
Marion, OH 43306
$67/yr

Library Hi Tech and
Library Hi Tech News
Pierian Press
Box 1808
Ann Arbor, MI 48106
$98/yr

Library Software Review
Meckler Corporation
11 Ferry Lane West
Westport, CT 06880
203-226-6967
$69.50
    This journal offers a multitude of articles, book an
software reviews, and news of technology relevant t
libraries.

Public Computing
Meckler Corporation
    The journal of public-access microcomputing is n
longer a separate publication, but is now incorporated int
Small Computers In Libraries.

Small Computers In Libraries
Meckler Corporation
11 Ferry Lane West
Westport, CT 06880
203-226-6967
$29.50
    This is the original journal of its kind, offerin
informative articles on hi tech areas as well a
down-to-earth topics.

echnicalities
1.E. Sharpe, Inc.
0 Business Park Drive
rmonk, NY 10504
14-273-1800
36

APPENDIX D:

Software Directories

The Book of Apple Software

Jeffrey Stanton, Mia McCroskey, and Michael Mellin's *The Book of Apple Software*, (Arrays, Inc.) is an annual publication that covers hundreds of programs, including productivity (word processing, database management, tele-communications, etc.), education, entertainment, graphics, utilities, and home/personal. Vendor list and index included. Programs are all given a thorough evaluation, including a grading system of different criteria (overall rating, ease of use, reliability, value for money, and documentation). $24.95 (6th edition).

The Book of Adventure Games I & II

The Book of Adventure Games (Arrays, Inc.), by Kim Schuette, covers a type of software that is typically known as interactive fiction. These games generally have their own small world, sometimes with graphics and sometimes all-text. Players wander around trying to open doors, solve puzzles, escape being eaten by grues, and score points by doing so. The solutions are given along with a review of each games. Nearly all have Apple versions. A third volume was recently published. $19.95.

Directory of Microcomputer Software

Directory of Microcomputer Software (DataPro) comes bound in a looseleaf binder since monthly updates must be inserted and old pages removed. This subscription service is huge, and it does cover many general areas and gives most data such as price, warranty, and vendor. Approximately four thousand software packages are entered, many of

which have Apple versions. While annotations do not appea
to be critical, they are descriptive and do not appear to b
simply catalog notes. $550 first year, $420 thereafter.

Apple Software for Pennies

Bertram Gader, and Manuel V. Nodar have published
volume, *Apple Software for Pennies*, listing two thousan
free programs for your Apple. None of them appear to b
library-specific, but there are business products listed wit
where and how they may be acquired. $9.95.

Catalogs

There is one other excellent source of softwar
information, the *Software Publishers' Catalogs Annua*
(Meckler Corporation). Over two thousand software catalog
are reproduced on microfiche, along with a printed index
Sixty-five subject headings are used. Price of 1986 editio
was $165.

APPENDIX E:

Apple or General Microcomputer User Groups

Alabama

outh Alabama Users Group
ox 8894
Mobile, AL 36608

MAUG
520 Ridgeland Road East
Mobile, AL 36609

Arizona

Adam 2 Apple Users Group
ox 34056
Phoenix, AZ 85067
02-277-8511

Arkansas

West Helena Microcomputer User's Group
ox 2184
West Helena, AR 72390

California

an Leandro Apple Easters Users Group
ob Shayler
200 Bancroft Avenue
an Leandro, CA 94577

outh Bay Computer Education Group
675 Torrance Blvd., Suite 202
Torrance, CA 90503

Technical Users Group
Box 705
Van Nuys, CA 91408

Colorado

Computer C.A.C.H.E.
8692 E. Hampden Avenue
Box 255
Denver, CO 80231

Connecticut

Connecticut Computer Society
Montevideo Road
Avon, CT 06001

Woodbury Computer Club
c/o Woodbury Library
Main Street
Woodbury, CT 06798

Delaware

Franklin/Apple Users Group
c/o Software Kingdom, Inc.
512 N. Dupont Hwy
Dover, DE 19901

Florida

Adam User Group
4757 #B Sunny Palm Circle
West Palm Beach, FL 33415

Apple Computer Enjoyment Society
Box 291557
Ft. Lauderdale, FL 33329

WB Apple Apple Users Group
03 Devon Court
Wright, FL 32548

Gainesville Apple Peelers
330 SW 13th Street
Gainesville, FL 32608

Space Coaster Apple Users Group
Box 2112
Merritt Island, FL 32952

Illinois

C.A.C.H.E. (Umbrella group with many
     special interest groups)
23 S. Franklin #804
Box C-176
Chicago, IL 60606

CIA User Group
Box 1462
Peoria, IL 61602

Kentucky

Owensboro Microcomputer User Group
1841 Bonnie Castle Drive
Owensboro, KY 42301

New Hampshire

Southern New Hampshire Apple Core
Drawer 3647
Nashua, NH 03061

New Jersey

Apple Jack
c/o Leanna Povilatitis
Box 634
Madison, NH 07940

New Mexico

Applequerque Computer Club
Box 35508
Albuquerque, NM 87176

New York

Computers Anonymous
PSC Box 1499
APO, NY 09130

Rochester Apple Cider
Box 40562
Rochester, NY 14604

Southern Tire Apple Core
c/o Earle Naumann
Ely Park Apt. X-4
Binghamton, NY   13905
607-729-0708

Pennsylvania

Apple Army
RD1 Box 83 1/2
Dornsife, PA 17823

Tennessee

Music City Apple Core
120 Credstmoor, Suite 333
Nashville, TN 37215

Vermont

Green Mountain Apple Club
/o Steve Hirsch
85 North Avenue Apt. 87
Burlington, VT 05401

APPENDIX F:

SLS Microcomputer Survey

⎧is survey is appended as an example of how to obtain
d organize useful data about microcomputer use in a
⎧rary system. Many library groups, even statewide, have
⎧oduced such listings with excellent results. Anyone who
eds to know may look in the index for a library using
⎧rdware or software which is being considered for
⎧rchase or with which they are having difficulty and then
ll the library for a reference or for help. A printed
py should be distributed since an online or electronic
rsion will be accessible to only a small percentage of the
⎧tential users, and to an even smaller number of those
⎧o have not yet purchased a microcomputer. Such a
rvey typically takes only 2 to 5 hours to produce and
stribute, depending upon the size of the system or area
⎧ing covered.

These are the results taken from a survey of libraries
Illinois.

SLS Microcomputer Survey

(Library and Equipment Listing)

1. Acorn Public Library District

2 Apple IIe (two drives each)
Imagewriter Printer
Apple Daisy Wheel Printer
Contact: Denise Webber (687-3701)

AppleWorks
- Word processing: Boa
  minutes, form lette
  contracts, agendas, auc
  letters, Board resolutio
  policy changes, flyers, etc
- Spreadsheet: Many payr
  functions, budget, sala
  schedules.

Pinpoint
- Calendar, calculato
  spellcheck

Newsroom
- New for newsletters

LibraryWorks
- Acquisitions

2. Bellwood Public Library

Apple IIe, 128K, Duodisc Drive,
Hayes Smartmodem 1200
NEC Spinwriter 3550 printer
Contact: Robert A. Harris (547-7393)

AppleWorks 1.2
- used for general typi
  chores: job descriptio
  procedure manuals, boa
  reports and minutes, e
  ployment applicatior
  "balancing" deposit mon

	against videotapes checked out, serials lists, lists of community groups. Have created templates. No spreadsheet use.
int Shop	- (with Printshop Companion and Graphics Library Discs 1 and 3) for posters, signs, banners.
›ple Access 1.0	- Used to communicate with SAVS and Robert F. White (Payroll Service) computers.

Blue Island Public Library

›ple IIe, 64K, Dos 3.3, two drives
›ple II3, 128K, ProDOS, two drives
.gital Equipment Corp LA-50 Dot Matrix
›ntact: Jay Wozny (388-1078)

| ›pleWorks | - word processing; financial (but no payroll or inventory), only use statements; database use, Zone 7 large print lists |
| ›ant Cards | - card production |

Broadview Public Library

›ple IIc, 128K two disk drives
›ple 1200 Modem, Silver Reed exp 500 printer
›ntact: Bonnie Schwanz (345-1325)

›pleWriter IIe	- video lists, video descriptions, job descriptions, circ. manual, correspondence
›pleWorks 1.3	- new (not used yet)
·int Shop	- (used with different dot matrix printer) banners and signs

CLSI MSS backup   - backup when CLSI is dow

5. Calumet City

Apple IIc, 64K, two disk drives
Okidata 72 printer
Contact: Vickie Novak (862-6220)

Avant Cards   - Catalog cards
Print Shop   - Posters, flyers

Apple IIe, 1-mb RAM, two disk drives
Daisy Wheel printer

AppleWorks

Apple IIe, 64K, two disk drives

AppleWorks
CLSI MSS   - CLSI Backup

6. Chicago Ridge Public Library

Televideo 816, 64K, 23-mb hard drive
Televideo 802, 64K 20-mb hard drive
Televideo 800A, 64K
Hayes Smartmodem 300 & 1200 baud modems
Qume Sprint 11/23 printer
Contact: Mark West (423-7753)

SAM
 (Simple Answer Machine)   - Catalog and circulation
WordStar   - Word processing & Email
CalcStar   - Report generation/
                                 Budgeting

Standard Brand PC, 640K, 20-mb hard drive

BiblioFile   - Cataloging
Anybook   - Order information

andy 1000, 10-mb hard drive, Radio Shack Line Printer VI
eskmate   - Accounting

Cicero Public Library

pple II+, two disc II drives, ERA II (by Microcom) modem,
pson II (MX-80 II F/T) printer

pple IIc, Imagewriter II printer
ontact: David Thaw (652-8084)
    Computer runs original program for lists (e.g., video
patron computer software). Communications software is
sed to access CLSI, SAVS, DIALOG. A reader's advisory
le is planned to be put on PFS:File.

rint Shop   - signs, banners

Concordia College

300 OCLC workstation
ontact: Henry R. Latzke (771-8300 x450)

Darien Public Library

Apple IIc, 64K
Apple drives
pple printer
ontact: Betty Hughes (960-2566)

vant Cards   - catalog cards
PI Accounting program   - accounting

). Dolton Public Library District

eneric IBM XT, 640K
mdek 310A printer
ontact: Ginger Miloserny (849-2385)

WordStar 3.3   - Word processing
BiblioFile   - Cataloging
IBM AT, 512K, 20-mb hard disk, 1 floppy
Texas Instruments Omni 800 Model 865 printer
Contact: Fran Krysek (849-2385)

Metafile   - accounting and payroll
WordStar   - Word Processing
SuperCalc III Ver. 2.1   - Spreadsheet

11. Downers Grove South High School ICM

Apple IIe, 128K, 2 disk drives
Okidata Microline 92 printer
Contact: Barbara Pray (852-0600)

DB Master   - AV equipment inventory
                                 computer disk inventory
                                 indexing collective bi
                                 graphy and magazine
Bookends   - Indexing yearbooks
Card   - Catalog cards

IBM PC XT, 256K, 2 disk drives
Hayes Smartmodem
Epson MX185

Smartcom   - Communications to SLS
DB Master   - Overdues, bibs, paperbac
                                 inventory, magazines

12. Elmhurst College, A.C. Buehler Library

IBM PC, 320K, 2 IBM drives
Hayes Smartmodem
Hewlett-Packard Laser Jet Printer
Contact: Janette Trofimuk (279-4100 x255)

WordStar 2000 2.0   - Bibliographies
Lotus 1-2-3   - Subject list of periodicals
dBase III Plus 1.0   - Database management

martcom II   - Communications

3. Elmhurst Public Library

pple IIe, 36K, 2 Apple Drives
ayes Smartmodem 1200
BM Personal Computer Graphics Printer
ontact: Raita Vilnins or Marylou Kutchka

    Used primarily for online searching

uick File   - budget   and   personnel
                                    information

BM PC XT, 256K, 1 floppy and hard disk
pson FX-80
ontact: Raita Vilnins or Sylvia Yeh (279-8696)

ordStar 2000   - Booklists,   procedure
                                    manuals
Base III+   - Mailing   lists, periodicals
                                    files
otus 1-2-3   - Budget, etc.

BM PC XT, with 20-mb hard disk
itizen MSP 10 printer

inder 4.0   - Index local newspaper

4. Frankfort Public Library

pple IIe (expanding with RamWorks)
 floppy drives
nagewriter printer
ontact: Pat McCarthy (815-469-2423)

ppleWorks   - Accounting   functions,
                                    periodical holdings, applica-
                                    tion forms, etc.

15. Grande Prairie Public Library

Kaypro PC-10, 640K, 20-mb hard disk, 1 floppy drive
Citizen MSP-10 printer
Contact: Gordon Welles (798-5563)

WordStar	- Word processing
Print Shop	- Banners and signs
SuperCalc 3	- Statistical reports

16. Green Hills Public Library

Apple IIe, 64K, 2 Apple drives
U.S. Robotics 212A Modem
NEC Spinwriter 3510 printer

Avant Cards	- Catalog cards
AppleWriter	- Word processing
DB Master	- Mailing labels
BPI	- General Ledger
ASCII Express	- Telecommunications to access DIALOG and SAVS

17. Harvey Public Library

Compaq Deskpro 286, 640K, 2 built-in 360k drives
one built-in Compaq 20-mb hard disk drive
Hayes 1200 B Internal modem
IBM Proprinter
Contact: Glenn Kersten (331-0757)

Lotus 1-2-3 1.A	- Bookkeeping/ledger, and spreadsheet
WordStar 2000 1.01	- Word processing for reports, correspondence an bibliographies.
Newsroom	- (original version) for creating newsletters with graphics.
Sign Designer	- (original version) sign (var. sizes, 4 fonts)

Nutshell   - (original version) A data-
                                       base manager (not received
                                       yet), to be used

18. Hinsdale Public Library

Apple IIe, 64K, 2 Apple Drives
Apple Personal Modem
Apple Imagewriter (wide)

PFS:Write   - (MD-DOS   and   ProDOS
                                       vers.) periodical holdings
                                       list, quarterly newsletter,
                                       new book list, procedure
                                       manuals,   inventory   of
                                       equipment and furniture.
VisiCalc   - Technical services statistics
                                       (i.e., books and materials
                                       added and withdrawn each
                                       month), circulation, ILL, an
                                       reference monthly stats.

19. Hinsdale South High School

Apple IIe, 128K
2 floppies
NEC Spinwriter
Apple DMP
Contact: Mary Winiecki (887-1730 x250)

AppleWorks 1.3
Quick Card   - Catalog cards

IBM PC, 256K
2 floppies
ProPrinter IBM

RBase 5000
WordPerfect 4.0   - Word processing

20. Hodgkins Public Library District

Televideo TS-816/40, 128K
8-inch Winchester hard disk (33.20 mb)
Qume Spring 11.55 printer
Contact: Gayle S. Barr (579-1844 or 579-3335)

SAM
  (Simple Answer Machine)   - Public-access catalog
WordStar   - Word processing

Library also owns: Televideo TS802, 64K, 2 slim-line 5 inch floppies

21. LaGrange Area Dept of Special Education (LADSE)

IBM PC 64-640K
2 IBM Floppies
Ven-tel
IBM Personal Graphics Printer
Contact: K. Gavin (354-5730)

PC File   - Acquisitions

22. LaGrange Public Library

Kaypro II
Signalman Mark VII modem (Anchor Automation)
Diablo 620 printer

Perfect Writer   - Word processing
Perfect Filer   - Periodical   database   and
                                 various indexes of small
                                 collections
Perfect Speller   - Spelling checker
Perfect Calc   - Spreadsheets for circulation
                                 reports
Profit Plan   - Budget forecasting

23. LaGrange Memorial Hospital Medical Library

IBM Personal Portable, 256K, 2 floppies
IBM Proprinter
Contact: Pat Grundke (579-4040)
Lotus 1-2-3

24. MacNeal Hospital/Health Sciences Resource Center

IBM XT, 64K, 1 drive
Hayes Smartmodem 1200 modem
Texas Instruments Omni 800 (model 855) and IDS Prism 80
printers
Contact: Rya Ben-Shir

FILLS	- Interlibrary loan
WordPerfect 4.1	- Word processing
Lotus 1-2-3	- Budget
VisiCalc 4.1	- Budget
WordStar	- Word processing
dBase II 2.30	- Library management
PC Talk	- Online database searching
Smartcom	- " "
Crosstalk	- " "
EasyLink	- " "

25. Matteson Public Library

2 Apple IIe, 128K, 2 Apple drives
TI Silent 700 printer and modem
Imagewriter printer
Epson LX80 printer

AppleWorks

26. Maywood Public Library

Apple IIe (3)
Apple II+ (1)
Contact: Patrick R. Dewey (343-1847)

PieWriter	- Word processing (reports, correspondence, etc.)
ASCII Express	- SAVS, Lincolnet, ALAnet
Print Shop	- Flyers, posters, etc.
Certificate Maker	- Children's programs
Librarian's Helper	- Catalog cards
WordPerfect	- Word processing
Smartcom II	- ALAnet, Lincolnet

27. Moraine Valley Community College

Apple IIe, 128K, 2 disk drives
Hayes 1200 modem
DEC Correspondent printer
Contact: Betsey Teo (974-4300 x223)

PFS:Write	- Word processing

IBM M300, 2 disk drives
Diablo 1650 printer

OCLC software	- Cataloging and processing

AT&T PC 5300, 2 disk drives
IBM Quietwriter printer

WordPerfect 4.1	- Word processing

28. Morton College

IBM PC, 256K, IBM dual disk drive
Hayes Smartmodem 1200
Epson LQ 1500 printer
Contact: Debbie Bocian (656-8000 x320)

Smartcom II 2.1	- Communications
WordStar 2.0	- Word processing

29. Nancy L. McConathy Public Library District

Apple IIe, 128K, 2 disk drives
Imagewriter II printer
Contact: Mary Frances Pena (757-4771)

AppleWorks	- Word processing, payroll and disbursements
Library List	- Booklists, reference searches on general topics
Print Shop	- Posters, banners, graphics

30. Oak Lawn Public Library

IBM XT PC, DOS 3.10, 640K, Bernoulli Box with 2 drives
(Bernoulli Box is a cartridge hard drive)
Toshiba P1350 printer
Contact: Linda Besbekos, Administrative Secretary
(422-4990)

MultiMate Advantage	- Word processing for library programs, policies, meeting notes, etc.
Open Systems Accounting System 3.0	- Accounts payable, general ledger, operating statement and balance sheet
Lotus 1-2-3	- will be used for statistical purposes
Fast Back	- Back up program

31. Oak Park Public Library

Apple II+, 64K
Hayes 1200 modem
Zenith 158, 640K
Hayes 1200B modem
Zenith 151, 640K
M300, 256K
Printers: Diablo 630, Epson FX85, Epson FX286, Epson
RX100

Contact: Marlene H. Ogg, Head of Technical Services
(383-8200 x28)
OCLC Terminal Software and Cataloging Microenhancer
Champion Accounting Software

DTI Serials Control 4.0   - Periodicals check-in
WordStar 3.0   - Word processing
SuperCalc 3, Release 2   - Statistics   and   financial
                             reports
PFS:File and Report   - File management
Smartcom II   - Communication
ASCII Express   - Communication
Cards   - Catalog cards

Contact: Lee Eagan/Candy Smith (442-6366)

Apple II+
CLSII Backup

32. Oak Park River Forest High School

IBM PC
2 IBM floppies
Epson FX-85 Printer
Contact: Joyce Leark (383-0700 x2097)

Symphony   - Rental films list & budget
                           - Previews
                           - Inventory
                           - Word processing
                           - Spreadsheet
                           - Database applications

Apple IIe
2 Apple floppies
Contact: Jean Schaubel (383-0700)

33. Park Forest Public Library

Apple IIe, 512K, 2 Apple drives
Hayes Smartmodem 1200

Printex 910 printer
Contact: Marcella Lucas (748-3731)

Avant Cards	- Catalog cards
Multiplan	- Library collection holdings, technical services staff sched.
Word Juggler 2.8.3	- Periodical holdings list (annual)
AppleWorks	- Word processing Organization list
Mailroom	- Mailing labels for Friends

4. Richton Park Public Library

Apple IIe, 64K, 2 Apple drives
Daisywriter Printer
Contact: Pat Nevins (481-5333)

AppleWriter   - Word processing

Also use a catalog card program produced by Mark West

5. Ridgewood High School IMC

Apple IIe, 256K, 2 Apple drives
Imagewriter printer
Contact: Cheryl Flinn (456-5880 x256)

Catalog Card Maker III	- Catalog cards, book pocket labels, circulation cards, booklists
AppleWorks	- Film orders, bibs, word processing

6. River Forest Public Library

IBM PC, 256K
2 floppies
Hayes 1200 baud modem
NEC P7 printer

Contact: Barbara Hall (366-5205)

Computer just installed - no software yet

37. Riverdale Public Library

Kaypro 4, 64K RAM (with 256K RAM Disk)
Contact: Jim Steenbergen (841-3311)

WordStar	- General Correspondenc with "Fancy Font" ver 2. (CP/M) to prepare typese copy
Superterm	- with ALAnet, SAVS data base booking, Lincolnet
Perfect Calc	- Financial reports fo Library and Friends Board
Perfect Filer	- Board, staff and Friend Boards lists, committee mailing lists
SCS Draw ver. 1	- for graphics
Graf ver. 3.0	- for line, bar and pie chart or statistical reports
Datemate 2.0	- to prepare montly an annual calendars for staf and Board.

Kaypro 10, 64K, 1 floppy disk drive, 1-mb 10 hard disk
Racal-Vadic VA 212LC 300/1200 modem
IBM Wheelwriter 5 printer
Contact: Jim Steenbergen

WordStar	- General correspondence minutes, policies
Perfect Calc	- Statistical reports t Board, output measures and Chamber of Commerc and Friends membershi lists, alphabetical list o vendors/disbursements

Apple IIe, 128K, duodisk drive

rintek 910 printer
ontact: Barb Diehl (841-3311)

vant Card	- Catalog cards
ppleWorks	- Monthly figures, spread-sheets, databases, etc.
ibliography Writer	- Patron bibliographies

3. Riverside Public Library

aypro 10
pson FX80 printer
ontact: Steven Oldert (442-6366)

ordStar	- Word processing

ontact: Ginny Kovalsky/Elinor Hackett (442-6366)

pple IIc
disk drives
EC Spinwriter 3510

racks magazine collection (no software listed)

BM PC, 640K
IBM Floppies
pson FX 80 printer
ontact: Judy Vokac (383-0700 x2395)

ymphony	- Keeps lists and does all accounting and financial record keeping for depart-ment

pple IIe
Apple Floppies
rother HR15 printer
.Itoh STarwriter F10 printer
ontact: Judy Vokac (383-0700 x2395)

uick Card	- Catalog cards
ppleWriter	- Word processing

PFS: File and Report   - Bibliographies, class set
                          AV software, etc.

39. Rosary College

IBM PC, 2 disk drives
Towa Daisywheel printer
Contact: Karen Becker(366-2490 x331)

PC Write   - Word processing
WordStar   - Word processing
Print Shop   - Graphics
Micro Con   - Retrospective conversion
Lotus 1-2-3   - Bookkeeping

40. Theodore Lownik Library, Illinois Benedictine College

M300 Workstation, 640K, 1 floppy drive
10-mb hard disk
Paradyne LSI 24 modem
Starwriter CItoh F10-40
Contact: Julia Hopewell (960-1500 x858)

WordPerfect   - Word processing

Apple IIe, 128K, 2 drives
AppleWriter modem
Contact: Julia Hopewell (960-1500 x858)

Homeword   - Word processing

41. West Suburban Hospital Medical Center Professiona
Library

Apple IIe, 2 Apple drives
Apple modem
Imagewriter printer
Contact: Julia B. Faust (383-6200 x6501)

DB IV   - Online card catalog
AppleWriter   - Word processing

pple Access II   - Telecommunications

2. West Suburban Hospital Health Information Center

3M PC, 256K
ayes Smartmodem 1200
3M Proprinter
ontact: Eva Eisenstein (383-6200 x6996)

rosstalk   - Communications   for
                                    searching
uick Card   - Catalog cards
FS:Write   - Word processing
FS:Plan   - Library statistics

3. Westlake Community Hospital

pple II+
ayes Micromodem
pson MX-80 (1)
ontact: Carol D. Strauss (681-3000 x3215)

ppleWriter II   - Reports, routing slips, SDI
                                    mailing labels, etc.
ata Capture   - Searches on BRS,
                                    Lincolnet, etc.

4. Westmont Public Library

 Apple IIe, 2 drives each
pple Personal Modem
 Apple Dot Matrix Printer, 1 Printek 910
ontact: Moira Buhse/Mary Simpson (969-5625)

ppleWorks   - Library budget
rint Shop   - Library graphics
Jewsroom   - Library graphics
FS:File   - Database files for plays in
                                    collection, computer soft-
                                    ware lists, magazine inven-

Avant Cards	tory list - Catalog cards
Apple Access	- SAVS and Wilsonline

45. Willowbrook Public Library

Apple IIe, 2 drives
Epson printer
Contact: Nancy Ciesniewski (887-8760 or 887-8875)

Avant Cards	- Catalog cards
AppleWorks	- Word processing for librar documents, database fc mailing labels, spreadshec or financial report (future)
PFS:Write	- Word processing
Print Shop	- Posters, notices, etc.
MSS	- Backup for CLSI

46. Worth Public Library District

3 Apple IIe, single disk drive
Apple modem 1200
Imagewriter and Pentek printers
Contact: Jean Novelli (448-2855)

AppleWorks	- Spreadsheet for monthl' and yearly report of per cent of budget allocation: Database for bibs, vide coop. holdings, new book (3 months), Friends mailin; list, registered patron mailing/labels programs pamphlet shelf list, yearl' disbursements. Word pro cessor for memos, reports form letters.
Print Shop	- (with Printshop Companio and Printshop graphics

for signs and library and
organizational graphics.

Newsroom - In-house newsletter
AppleWriter - not used (use AppleWorks
instead.

INDEX

203-226-6967

A continuing series of practical volumes for librarians using Apple Computers for technical processing, public access, and administrative support.

Order Form

**Please enter my order for the following volume(s) of the ESSENTIAL GUIDE TO APPLE COMPUTERS
IN LIBRARIES:**

Series Editor: Jean Armour Polly
Series ISBN 0-88736-048-3

___ This is a standing order. Send each new title beginning with volume ___ as it is published at a 10% discount.

___ Volume 1: Public Technology: The Library Public
Access Computer
ISBN 0-88736-049-1

___ Volume 2: Hardware: Set-up and Expansion
ISBN 0-88736-075-0

each vol. **$ 24.95**

___ Volume 3: Communications and Networking
ISBN 0-88736-076-9

___ Volume 4: Software for Library Applications
ISBN 0-88736-077-7

___ Volume 5: The Library Macintosh
ISBN 0-88736-078-5

Name _____

Organization _____

Address _____

City _____ State _____ Zip _____

Purchase Order No. _____ Authorized Signature _____

□ Please bill my organization   □ Payment enclosed (required for personal orders)

BUSINESS REPLY CARD

FIRST CLASS PERMIT NO. 66   WESTPORT, CT.

POSTAGE WILL BE PAID BY ADDRESSEE

MECKLER PUBLISHING
11 FERRY LANE WEST
WESTPORT, CT 06880

ISBN 0-88736-077-7